The Banks

and

Risk Management

CAMBRIDGE SEMINAR 1988

The Banks

and

Risk Management

Based on the Seminar held at
Christ's College, Cambridge, 4–9 September 1988

The Chartered Institute of Bankers

10 Lombard Street, London EC3V 9AS

Chartered Institute of Bankers (CIB) Publications
Published under exclusive licence and royalty agreement by Bankers Books Ltd.

Copies can be obtained from:
THE CHARTERED INSTITUTE OF BANKERS
10 Lombard Street
London
EC3V 9AS

ISBN 0 85297 217 2

Cartoons by Ben Shailo
Cover design by John Robertson

Typeset in 10pt on 12pt Baskerville by McCorquodale Confidential Print Ltd.
Text printed on 100gsm Combat Economy Cartridge. Cover 240mic Astralux One Sided Card.
Printed and bound by McCorquodale Confidential Print Ltd. for Blades East and Blades Limited.

CONTENTS

ERIC GLOVER
Director, Cambridge Seminar 1988

Eric Glover started his career with Shell International in 1957, after taking a Classics degree at Oxford. He spent five years abroad, mainly in Borneo and Uganda, and joined the staff of the Institute on his return to England, in January 1963. He was Director of Studies from 1968 to 1982, and has been Secretary-General since then. He directed the International Banking Summer School at St. John's College, Cambridge, in 1985, and has already directed four Cambridge Seminars.

FOREWORD

We were very fortunate at this year's Seminar both in the choice of theme, which proved to be highly topical, and in finding four speakers of such experience and authority. Their papers form the main part of this book, and the case study and discussion syllabuses were written by the syndicate chairmen. I should like here to thank all of them for their contributions.

Since these seminars started, in 1968, we have always ensured that the proceedings would be of benefit to all our members, and not just the 100 or so who attended the week at Christ's College. Publications such as this help our local centres in running their own events, and this year the major banks have already placed advanced orders, another indication of the importance of the issues discussed.

I hope that we may help all readers to understand some of the mysteries of the rapidly changing environment in which they work, and therefore to be in a better position to face the challenges which lie ahead.

ERIC GLOVER
Director, Cambridge Seminar 1988

Rodney D Galpin, FCIB

Rodney Galpin entered the Bank of England in 1952. After a series of progressively more senior appointments, including a period as Secretary to the then Governor, Lord Cromer, he became an Executive Director in 1984 with responsibility for Operations and Services. By 1987 his portfolio included Banking Supervision and Banking Operations. From 18 July 1988 he became Chairman-Designate of Standard Chartered Bank.

Mr Galpin has wide interests. He is, among other things, a Companion of The British Institute of Management; a freeman of the City of London; a member of INSEAD's UK Advisory Board; a Life Governor of his old school, Haileybury & Imperial Service College (now known simply as Haileybury); a member of the Council of The Scout Association; and an Honorary Steward at Westminster Abbey.

Rodney D Galpin, FCIB

1. A CENTRAL BANKER'S VIEW

Contents

BANK
GOVERNOR

AN IMPRUDENT LENDER OF FIRST RESORT
VISITS THE LENDER OF LAST RESORT

A CENTRAL BANKER'S VIEW

Introduction

It is as well that I should start by defining more precisely the ground which this paper is intended to cover.

Central banks exist in most countries – some are institutions of relatively recent origin; others, like the Bank of England, have much longer histories. None, however, can claim an existence as a central bank which pre-dates the formation of commercial banks. They have varied responsibilities, in many cases different in a number of respects one from another. This owes much to the nature of their origin. It is, of course, true that all have a concern for the viability of the banking system in their own country, but many have no formal role in the regulation of banks, this being a responsibility in the hands of another official, as opposed to private, body separately staffed and administered and outside the control of the central bank. In the United Kingdom, the Bank of England, the central bank, has been statutorily entrusted with the regulation of banks, as defined in legislation.

It is from the perspective of a regulator that this paper is written and I am not proposing to address at any length other, and perhaps more universal, characteristics of a central bank's responsibilities. These may in some cases be thought to have the potential for conflict with a regulator's role and it would be confusing – and perhaps even in conflict with the aims of the organisers of this seminar – to expand my canvas to accommodate such considerations. The thoughts in this paper might therefore be best described as providing "a central bank *regulator's* view".

The origins of the Bank of England and its Regulatory Function

I should like to remind you briefly of the origins of the Bank of England and the development of its regulatory function. The two are linked and the former has influenced the style of regulation practised by the Bank of England.

The Bank of England was established by a Scotsman in 1694. The money provided by the subscribers for shares was lent to the then Government and was used to finance the war against France. The Bank was nevertheless a privately-owned institution, though created under Royal Charter, and so it remained until 1946 when it was nationalised – the first institution to be brought into public owner-ship in this way. It clearly had close links with the Government but they were not proprietors, rather borrowers. It obtained over the years certain privileges under Act of Parliament, most notably the position of being the sole note-issuing authority in England. The Bank was encouraged to compete with other banks to maximise its profits and increasingly, as the years progressed, to perform a variety of rescue operations. By the early 1800s, the Bank had agreed to open discount accounts for the money market to which it would lend against the security of bills of exchange. In the interests of risk management, it naturally began to take an interest in the affairs of these customers and their clients whose bills were held as security. It began in other words to regulate, in its own self-interest, the money market houses. Business pressures from time to time led to a level of bankruptcies which excited the interest of politicians, as well as the Bank's internal management, and by the middle of the 19th century it had become customary, though not without reluc-tance on the Bank's part, for the Government to seek to persuade the Bank to do what it could to alleviate such pressures. It was not, however, until the Baring crisis of 1890 that the Bank mounted and organised its first co-operative rescue to deal with a banking crisis. The Government resisted playing a part since they would have to answer for it in Parliament, which the Bank as a privately-owned institution would not. The Bank had thus by then, for the protection of its own balance sheet and those of a wider constituency, mostly represented on its own Court of Directors, begun to concern itself with regulation. Other institutions had begun to recognise that the Bank was useful to them; it was close to Government and influential through its activities (particularly as the sole bank of issue); it understood banking since it was a bank itself and its Directors, all non-executive, were drawn from the most prestigious of the merchant banks in London. Because it had accepted this role voluntarily, without there being any legal requirement to do so, it could act flexibly and with understanding, which made it all the more acceptable to those whose affairs it chose to monitor.

This flexible and voluntary arrangement continued until the passing of the Banking Act 1979, which for the first time introduced a comprehensive and statutory basis for bank regulation. Clearly by then the list of those in whose activities it was interested had widened, but the extension had been somewhat haphazard, taking place under the influence of events or in connection with the exercise of other functions, such as monetary policy, associated with the Bank of England's central banking role.

The Need for Supervision

In the same way that there developed over the years the acceptance that there were certain responsibilities which it was appropriate for a central bank to undertake, so has it now come to be accepted that banks need to be supervised. Both requirements would have seemed strange to our great grandfathers, for whom the concept of *caveat emptor* prevailed. It is interesting to consider why supervision of the banking system is now considered relevant and necessary. In my opinion the overriding influence has been that of consumer protection. As populations have become better educated and more sophisticated so has the banking habit spread. No longer is banking a cosy stable domestic club, conducted in a sort of village atmosphere similar to that of the traditional city, where all were close to and aware of the business ethics of others. In such a climate it was entirely possible, and appropriate, to rely for supervision on the standing in which the players were held one by another. "My word is my bond", the traditional motto of the City of London, was a much prized statement of business ethics. I shall comment in the next section of this paper on the changes which have occurred recently in banking; suffice it to say at this stage that the environment is now international and dynamic, the risks far more complicated and the conditions much more competitive. In this situation it is not surprising that consumer interests have become more dominant.

Special Characteristics of Financial Institutions

It may be argued that consumer interests are as great in other spheres of activity. This is of course true, but the interests are different – and they are, as we all know, taken care of differently through legislation introduced to set corporate standards and to ensure that customers get a fair deal. Why, one may ask, need one go further with financial companies than with other types of companies? The answer, I judge, lies in the different characteristics of financial companies and their role as intermediaries in the distribution of wealth. Taking a simple example: I do not think any of us would argue that the bankruptcy of a large industrial company, serious though it might be, would have such a serious impact as that of a large banking company! In the former case, the failure of a competitor would be seen by other companies in the same sector as an opportunity to increase market share, whereas in a banking situation the immediate reaction of a competitor would be to assess whether or not the problem would spread more widely – perhaps even to its own balance sheet. This is because banking is an activity heavily dependent on the confidence of its depositors, many of whom have their savings at risk and may be influenced by financial columns which are now more comprehensive in their coverage than ever before. Another factor is the dependence of banks one on another. They may be active in the interbank market, where the participants, though more sophisticated than the private depositor, have much the same interest in protecting the value of their assets. Lines can quickly be cut and acute liquidity pressures built up. As a result loans may be called in prematurely to the disadvantage of the borrower whose activities may well be highly beneficial to the economy. Thus the viability of the banking system is seen as crucial to the continuance of business efficiency and general economic well-being. It is not surprising, therefore, that Governments have seen it as right to cater for the protection of the system through legislation.

A new breed of technocrats has been created – that of bank regulators, of whose number I was, until recently, a member. Although country systems may be different in style there is a common intent behind all systems of regulations. It is not, as some may imagine, to guarantee that there will never be a bank failure, but rather to minimise this risk by ensuring that bank managements are required to focus on the risks they run. It is not the regulator's responsibility to take management decisions; that would be usurping the authority of those entrusted under company legislation with the running of the business.

Recent Developments

The next section of this paper will look at recent developments in the nature of banking and the influence which these have had, and are still having, on the regulatory approach. I do not intend to go into the technical detail surrounding these changes. They will probably have touched you all. It is, however, worth listing the developments that have occurred and pointing to the reasons why change has arisen.

The first, and perhaps most fundamental, development has been the breakdown of functional distinctions between banks and other institutions. Traditionally banks were involved as intermediaries – they still are but no longer is this role seen as always necessary. The bigger companies have been able, because of higher credit ratings than banks, to borrow more cheaply in their own name than through the intermediation of a bank. Furthermore, business activities which previously had characterised banks, and banks alone, are now performed by a range of other companies, not all of which could be classed as financial institutions. Much, therefore, of the banks' traditional business, profitable in the past, has been lost to them. It is a moot point whether or not, with the internationalisation of corporate activity, this would have occurred if banks had been able to maintain their ratings with the credit agencies. But they have not because of the problems, most particularly sovereign debt exposure, which banks have faced.

Deregulation

Coupled with this change has been the process of deregulation. It is, as you will realise, something of a misnomer to describe this process as deregulation. It is rather a process of reregulation, since its effect has not been to do away with regulation but rather to intensify it, albeit in a different way by the introduction of new supervisory requirements. The term deregulation is, however, fairly used if by use of it one is seeking no more than to convey the freedom to compete which has arisen from the tendency for activities hitherto the characteristic of banks to be undertaken also by a range of other institutions.

Competition

Not only have banks had to face competition from other institutions. They have also faced it from other banks, many of which are now more international by nature. Business has had to be fought for as corporate customers, particularly if they are any size, look for the best financial package they can get. Corporate treasurers are more sophisticated clients! Less profitable opportunities, greater client sophistication, wider competition all flow through in their effect to the bottom line of a bank's balance sheet. The latter has also been affected by pressures on the adequacy of bank capital – a feature highlighted by the provisions that have had to be made by banks against their sovereign debt exposure. But there have been other difficult situations also – for instance in the United States, real estate, energy and agriculture.

This catalogue will, I hope, serve to explain why it was almost inevitable that new financial instruments should be introduced, many of them off-balance sheet and thus not constrained by capital adequacy.

New Technology

At the same time, new technology has been developed and introduced. The impact of this has not yet been fully felt, though it has for many of us considerably changed the pattern of working life. Some new instruments are heavily dependent on computer technology, and software exists which assists in the management of the risks. Many banks, in the process of deregulation, have ventured into the securities business and have had to learn to understand the different types of risk which can attend securities dealing or underwriting a dealing portfolio. The assessment of credit risk has been the traditional role of the banker, and some have argued that the changes described above imply that credit risk assessment will no longer be undertaken – to the detriment of the financial system as a whole. And, as stated earlier, some banks are certainly more concerned these days with a wider range of risks than just credit or counterparty risk – position risk, settlement risk and interest rate risk are now common enough features of risk management.

An additional ingredient has been the growth of globalised banking, in which technology has also helped. It is not unusual these days for an international bank to operate a 24 hour dealing or foreign exchange portfolio passing positions from centre to centre as the world rotates. Banks have, of course, always been concerned about counterparty risk but these risks must now be as great as ever and can, in the long run, only be accurately monitored and controlled through the introduction of real time systems, able to assess a bank's exposures on a global basis.

Changes in the Regulatory Environment

I now wish to concentrate on the changes in the regulatory environment to which the factors I have outlined have contributed. I will start with the domestic UK scene and then comment on the international aspects.

I referred earlier to the fact that it was not until the Banking Act of 1979 that the Bank of England was given statutory powers to supervise banks. This legislation introduced for the first time in the United Kingdom a statutory definition of a bank. Previously legislation affecting companies engaged in the business of banking had been of a piece-meal nature, directed towards individual aspects of a banking business rather than its whole, and could be found in specific sections of various Acts of Parliament, only a few of which (eg the Exchange Control Act and The Control of Borrowing Order) were adminstered by the Bank. It was always likely that the first Banking Act would need amendment as experience of its workings was gained. This turned out to be the case and a new Banking Act came into effect last year.

The new Act gave the Bank of England more extensive powers. It did away with the two-tier system (of licensed deposit takers and recognised banks) which had characterised the 1979 Act. This distinction, which gave the Bank greater powers over the former than the latter group, had come to be seen, most visibly in the Johnson Matthey Bankers affair, as mistaken. New also in the Act – and significant – is the establishment of a Board of Banking Supervision to advise on banking regulation, and requirements for the involvement of auditors more formally in the supervisory process through the auditing of systems and controls. Arrangements have also been introduced whose purpose it is to limit, other than in exceptional circumstances, any single or connected exposure to a maximum of 25% of a bank's capital. The role of non-executive directors and the establishment of Audit Committees within banks also feature in the new guidelines issued by the Bank of England.

I should here mention, in parenthesis, some features of both this and the former Banking Act which, while not unique, are not followed in all countries. The UK legislation – the Act itself – has been drafted in general rather than specific terms. Specific requirements – in effect the interpretation of the general requirements – are a matter for the Bank of England and are issued in the form of notices and guidelines. This approach enables the Bank to amend its regulatory approach and introduce new features, without primary legislation, for which in a busy parliamentary schedule it may be difficult to find time. It means also that regulation can more easily be kept up to date and as a result be adapted fairly quickly to changing practice or innovation in the market place. Such an approach additionally makes it possible for the Bank to produce its guidelines through a consultative process with the banking industry – a process which is designed to ensure as far as possible that the regulator's approach and requirements reflect the realities of how business is done and measure the risks involved in a manner acceptable, or at least not wholly foreign, to bank managements.

The Measurement of Risk

It is not the regulator's purpose to frustrate sound and profitable business. His concern is essentially with the measurement of risk, and the changes to which I have already referred, which are reflected in the new Banking Act, have this consideration as their rationale. The abolition of the two-tier system has resulted in a standard approach to risk for all supervised institutions. Regulation is not, however, just a matter of applying financial ratios – it needs to be balanced with judgments about the ability of individual managements to run the particular, perhaps specialised, business in which they are involved. While we had a two-tier system, with its status implications, the pressure to move into the first division became for some a reason to develop banking services for which they had no expertise and thus to increase the risks run by the business.

Through the creation of the Board of Banking Supervision – a body of whom the majority of members are bankers, lawyers or accountants – there has become available to the Bank of England a source of practical experience in risk taking. Not many of those involved in the day to day business of bank regulation have practical experience of banking and undoubtedly the input of the Board brings a new dimension to the Bank's approach. This, I would suggest, is of as much benefit to the banking industry as it is to the Bank itself.

The new emphasis on large exposures policy, Audit Committees, non-executive directors and the role of auditors can all be justified on the grounds that, effectively used, such developments should help bank managements in the recognition of, and control over risks, in their individual businesses. If banking was a risk-free business there would be no need for its regulation. New risks are now being undertaken and it is a challenge both for management and the regulator to understand them. While there may be differences of view as to the weightings employed there is no dissent,

for instance, to the view that off-balance sheet activities carry some
measure of risk, and the potential for loss and impairment of capital.
Hence the Bank of England's decision some years ago to apply a
capital requirement against note issuance and revolving under-
writing facilities.

International Aspects of Banking Regulation

I now turn to the international aspects of banking regulation. The
United Kingdom's entry into Europe, and the banking crisis of the
mid 1970s, were both factors which contributed to the growth of
international co-operation in this area. The Treaty of Rome looks
for the removal of competitive distortions between banks and
negotiations about the harmonisation of regulatory standards have
been a staple diet in Brussels. The banking problems of the 1970s
brought home to the authorities the growing internationalism of
banking and convinced them that no longer could banking problems be regarded as wholly insulated within the domestic economy.
The growing freedom of capital movements round the world
reinforced the wish for co-ordination and the Group of Ten
Countries decided, almost 13 years ago, to establish a Committee
located in Basle – and now known as the Cooke Committee – to
concentrate solely on regulatory issues. The prospect of co-
ordinating policies in a group of countries, whose banking systems
are all well developed and reflect the practice of domestic tradition,
was by no means easy – but the achievements of the Committee since
its inception are by no means inconsiderable. A relatively early
achievement was that of defining where regulatory responsibility
rested for a banking group which had branches and subsidiaries
worldwide. This led on to an acceptance that regulation should be
carried out on a consolidated basis and not restricted solely to the
domestic operations of the institution concerned. These achievements were reflected in a document, called the Basle Concordat, to
which many countries have now adhered.

   The most significant achievement, however, of The Cooke
Committee was to build, as they did last year, on an initiative taken
between the US authorities and the Bank of England, to introduce

common capital standards, through a risk asset-based system of capital measurement. As a result we are now on the road towards the removal internationally of some of the competitive distortions faced by international banking groups.

Securities Regulation

Arrangements to tackle similar problems are going to have to be introduced between security regulators. The challenge here is a large one but securities regulation cannot just be ignored by the banking regulator since, as pointed out previously, securities business is now being undertaken by many banking groups.

With the passing of the Financial Services Act and the extension of regulation to the securities industry the Bank of England has had over the recent past to consider how these requirements fit in with their own. Co-operation domestically between the Bank and the regulators of securities firms and other financial institutions has been allowed for in the legislation applying to both regulators. Such co-operation is already well developed bilaterally. So as to ensure that within a financial group there is no area which is so unregulated as to create a risk to the rest of the group, colleges of regulators have been formed: these will meet regularly at the instance of one of their number (the lead regulator) to review the financial state of the group as a whole. In this way the potential for regulatory underlap can be addressed.

Need for Harmony

There is of course also a danger in overregulation. Securities and banking regulators see capital requirements differently – the former being concerned that it should protect against short-term pressures, such as arose in October 1987, while the latter concentrates on the availability of liquidity to meet short-term pressures and sees capital in a bank as far more permanent than do the securities regulators. Regulatory requirements consequently differ and one of the challenges of the moment, as functional distinctions between financial institutions break down, is to operate the two approaches in harmony. This can readily enough be done if subsidiaries exist, since this effectively retains functional distinctions between separate parts of a single financial group. Subsidiarisation is not, however, a regulatory requirement and many banks, particularly in the merchant banking field, combine on one balance sheet business activities of both a banking and securities nature; and many have done so for years – underwriting being an example which springs to mind. A regulatory procedure is being constructed to deal with this problem, which if unaddressed would leave institutions having to submit information to more than one regulator, all of whom might be applying differing capital adequacy requirements against the same balance sheet. The procedure is to appoint one regulator – the one chosen is likely to be that for whom the predominant part of the business is most relevant – whose task it will be to receive supervisory information, make judgments about it and give to the other regulators, who have a more minor interest, a sort of "road worthiness" certificate. How effective, or flexible, this can be remains to be seen. It is clearly much more straightforward where, as in the Banking Act, the regulator is allowed to place reliance on the supervision of other regulators, but no such explicit provision exists – at any rate at present – in the Financial Services Act. One can well understand the dilemma faced by a regulator, entrusted by statute to fulfil a particular role, in relaxing his approach when to do so may leave him exposed to criticism, or worse, for having neglected his statutory duty.

An earlier section referred to international co-operation among banking regulators. International co-operation between securities regulators will be just as essential and has yet to get properly under way. It will be a significant challenge over the next few years to create such a forum and to address the regulatory issues in a way which will produce a convergence of approach.

Why, one may ask, is the convergence of regulatory standards necessary? So far, this paper has concentrated in large part on change, but it has also referred to competitive pressures. Both are factors which put bank managements under pressure. Where the management is competent no undue risk is probably being undertaken. Where the reverse is true risk must surely be increased.

The Interdependence of Banks

Banks are dependent in many ways one on another, perhaps as counterparties or, even more simply, as individual members of a constituency which depends upon confidence. There is therefore, as mentioned earlier, seen to be a need for their regulation. But need it be the same here as elsewhere? Here again competition and interdependence provide an answer. Competition is international. Differing regulatory standards distort competition and influence pricing, and it is strongly argued create playing fields slanted in favour of the least well regulated centres – ultimately to the risk of all the players. It is right to point out that, of course, it is not only regulatory requirements that can create such distortions in competition. National fiscal treatment or accounting practices can be just as effective as say monetary policy controls (eg in Japan), which regulate domestic rates of interest and control capital movements.

There are clearly interests of a conflicting nature between countries, and also banks, when it comes to judging what is, or what is not, an unfair competitive situation. There is, naturally enough, a lot of self-interest employed in coming to such judgments. Without firm views on the part of the authorities there would, one supposes, be a tendency to move towards the lowest common denominator in the process of evening out the bumps. This would be disastrous and ultimately make more likely a severe, and international, banking crisis. To avoid it will require give and take on all sides. It is interesting to note that the interdependence of banks is likely to be a factor in achieving the proper balance. Financial analysis of banking results, combined with steps to encourage greater disclosure in financial accounts, produce their own pressures on management. Results are more closely followed and the risks apparent in a bank's business can, and do, have an effect on its ability to trade. Taking these into account will encourage the commitment of management towards the minimisation of risks and the strengthening of its balance sheet, at least to the point when it no longer looks to be among the weaker brethren. The process will, of necessity, be somewhat slow.

Regulators, being part of a bureaucracy, will, however well meaning, have to avoid regulation for the sake of it. They will have to assess carefully the implications of the regulations they impose. In a domestic environment there would be little sense in a bureaucratic imposition of regulations which destroyed the capacity of their banks to compete with others, or which drove business important to their banks offshore. Such considerations will need to be weighed in the balance against the magnitude of the risks which the regulations are designed to minimise. The Bank of England is, I venture to submit, probably better equipped than others to make these assessments realistically. On the international front there will be some difficult issues to debate between those countries, like the United Kingdom, whose systems of regulation are less dirigiste and others who have traditionally had more of that approach. It will be interesting to see how much of the style of supervision in each country can be retained. That produces its own competitive advantages or disadvantages but it seems to me likely that it will be the countries with the strongest international position which are likely to be most influential in the debate. In this sense the United Kingdom is well placed.

Instruments of Regulation

I have said that it is the degree of risk incurred which should influence the detail of the regulatory approach. This is perhaps, therefore, the point at which to comment briefly on the instruments of regulation. The most important tool in a regulator's kit is the capital adequacy ratio. It is this which determines the capacity of the bank to trade and its ability to meet loss. Capital therefore needs to be certain; by which I mean it should be permanent and readily available when required. So you can expect the regulator to be firm and detailed in his requirements. Traditionally, capital was assessed against aggregated total assets as a trading multiplier. In the United Kingdom we have moved to a risk/assets ratio which assesses the adequacy of capital against the risks attached to the assets – a weighting formula general in its application to different classes of assets rather than specific to individual assets. This system has been accepted also throughout the Common Market and is a feature of the convergence proposals referred to earlier.

Another important tool is a liquidity requirement. In many countries banks are required to place balances with their central bank, usually for monetary control purposes. The use of special deposits in the United Kingdom fell into this category. From a regulatory viewpoint this is not strictly liquidity, since it may not readily be available to meet liquidity pressures nor does it necessarily vary in accordance with short-term liabilities/cash flow pressures. Instead it is usual to have regard to the matching profile of a bank's short-term assets and liabilities, supplemented perhaps by requirements (as mooted recently by the Bank of England) for each bank to hold a minimum level of specified high quality liquid assets in its portfolio as a stock of liquidity. Liquidity is the first line of defence against problems – its lack can quickly turn a problem of liquidity into one of insolvency.

Capital adequacy and liquidity are the essential ingredients of regulation. There are, however, other less formula-driven features. These are more concerned with the day-to-day management of the institutions supervised. They are, however, no less important. They are concerned with the quality of management in individual institutions and its ability to run prudently, honestly and successfully the business of the institution. These assessments take a variety of forms – some, such as, for instance, fitness and properness, being reflected in the detail of legislation as it affects directors and/or shareholder controllers, while others such as the systems and controls in place are matters for judgment by the regulators, aided (as is now written into statute in the United Kingdom) by the accounting profession. In the latter case, the reporting accountants, who incidentally may be different from the external auditors of the Bank, will have a responsibility to report on systems and controls, basing their judgments on detailed guidance issued by the Bank of England. Inadequate systems and controls create potentially serious risks for banks, and the accountants' reports are intended to draw the attention of both management and the regulators to deficiencies before they can begin seriously to affect the viability of the institution. It has been found necessary also in the United Kingdom to extend somewhat the criminal offences set out in the Banking Act. These cover among other things the taking of deposits without a licence and the provision of deliberately misleading information to the regulators. Other factors, such as the timeliness of returns, over-concentrated lending, large exposures policy, or procedures generally will be monitored by the regulators, particularly where they feel that deficiencies in practice are likely to carry with them potential for risk. Such monitoring may take place within the normal and regular supervisory interview; but it may also involve requests for special and additional information or returns – or even a visit by the regulators to the bank to look specifically, and in detail, at some aspect of the business. Judgments arrived at by the regulators are shared with the management of the institution.

To some extent it would seem from the comments above that the process of regulation is arbitrary in its application, or perhaps even discretionary. This is, indeed, the case in relation to the less important tests through which an institution is assessed, and it is right that it should be. Risks may for instance be greater in some institutions than in others; not all institutions undertake the same sort of business, nor are they all equally well managed. Regulators in the United Kingdom take pride in their flexibility, and it is in the interests of the banking community that regulation should be no more intrusive than is essential.

The Reality of the Market Place

It is not necessarily right that the regulator's view should always prevail. The consultative process used by the Bank of England is designed to assist in the development of a regulatory approach which reflects how business is actually done. Debate can, and does, take place during the period of policy formulation on the nature, extent and reality of the risks to which particular activities give rise. Unless the regulator reflects in his approach the reality of the market place, his influence to provide guidance will diminish and banks will tend to look more to the letter than the spirit of the law – and so far as London is concerned its position as a leading international financial centre would be diminished, to the disadvantage, it might be argued, of both the authorities and the banks which have seen fit to conduct business out of London.

Flexibility in regulation should not, however, lead to inconsistency or inequitable treatment. Not only would this involve the regulator in many cases in appeal procedures built into the Banking Act, but it would also destroy the trust and confidence which is a feature of the relationship in the United Kingdom between the regulated and the regulator.

Conclusion

In considering whether or not the regulator's role should always prevail one needs to underline that it is not his responsibility to take over the management of risks from the banks. He can give warnings, which one must admit will probably always be heeded, but subject to capital requirements a bank is free to make its own judgments. A history of poor judgment will, of course, increase the intensity of supervision and may well be reflected in the severity of the risk/assets ratio applied to a particular institution; but the decisions on individual risks remain firmly with management.

Banking is a risky business; it has become more so as innovation has occurred in response to competitive pressures. The business undertaken by banks is very different from the past – the risks are different. Just as management has had to react to these changes so has the regulator. The regulator, by the nature of his role, is reactive rather than proactive. If banks do not themselves recognise, and take prudent account of, the risks they run he will have to impose standards. How much better if banks can avoid undue risk and how appropriate, therefore, it is that The Chartered Institute of Bankers have chosen for the 1988 Cambridge Seminar the topic of risk management.

John A Brooks, FCIB

John Brooks is a Director and Deputy Group Chief Executive of Midland Bank Plc. He is also a Director of Thomas Cook Group and MasterCard International.

He joined the bank in 1949 at London's Bloomsbury branch, and the early stages of his career were spent in various domestic branch and Head Office positions. He was appointed General Manager (Computer Operations) in 1975, subsequently taking control of the bank's operations in the Midlands and South West. In February 1980 he was appointed a Director and assumed responsibility for the group's wholly owned operations in the British Isles, which included Clydesdale Bank, Forward Trust, the domestic operations of Midland Bank, Northern Bank and Thomas Cook. Then, in June 1985, in addition to his role as Deputy Group Chief Executive, he became responsible for the group's international activities and was particularly involved in the sale of Crocker National Corporation to Wells Fargo & Co. in 1986.

Currently, John Brooks is President of The Chartered Institute of Bankers. He is also a Companion of The British Institute of Management.

John A Brooks, FCIB

2. RISK IN DOMESTIC BANKING

Contents

[21]

COULD YOU ACCORD MY LOAN THIRD
WORLD STATUS ?

RISK IN DOMESTIC BANKING

"The art of banking is surely to know when to accept the risk. But first the able banker must be able to appreciate and assess that risk"
Mr L C Mather, The Lending Banker 1955

Introduction

The assumption and management of risk is of the very essence of the business of banking. The extent to which risk management is an art or a science, or indeed a judicious mixture of both, could form the subject of an interesting if inconclusive debate. There would however surely be little argument as to whether or not risk taking and risk management in banking require the deployment of special skills and judgment – for it is in this field that banking ability – of the individual or of the organisation – is most critically tested.

The traditional image of a domestic banker is that of the lending banker. Career progression in the large clearing bank branch networks was based upon gaining experience and demonstrating success in lending roles. The aspiration of every young banker was to progress from the operations and processing areas to the discreet calm of the managerial parlour.

In more recent years, of course, there have been enormous changes in our industry. The traditional skills of individual customer credit risk assessment remain as valid as ever, but today's bank managers must employ new techniques and have a wider perception of risk taking. The responsibility for running a business is being placed at much lower levels in the organisational pyramid than hitherto. The modern banker must be a businessman in a broader sense, coping with all the risks associated with managing a business enterprise in a rapidly evolving market place. His performance measurements are likely to include sales targets for a range of products, cost control criteria, resource management objectives and profit attainment, and all of this to be undertaken in an environment of fierce competition.

Risk then enters into many aspects of the management of our banking business. At board and executive management levels there is the ultimate responsibility of ensuring the protection and remuneration of the organisation's capital base with all the associated decisions on the timing and amount of external funding. Within the treasury area there are market risks arising from trading positions in currencies or assets, and the need to pitch any mismatching of maturities within prudent margins. Most importantly for a bank it is necessary to maintain liquidity of assets such that ability to meet any claims remains unquestioned in the eyes of depositors and third parties. There are also all the aspects of physical security – of premises and vault items – and also of the integrity of computer data.

I propose for the purposes of this paper to concentrate upon *credit* risk and deal with the other manifestations of risk management only to the extent to which they influence or are influenced by credit risk issues. The reasons for containing the scope of our examination in this fashion are:

— credit risk and credit risk-related issues are those which have the greatest impact on domestic line management at all levels.

— the many pressures which are placed upon domestic bankers reinforce the need to keep attention sharply focused upon credit risk in business development.

— the evolution of new credit risk assessment tools and techniques merit consideration.

— there are areas within the domestic banking market place which on credit risk grounds qualify for comment.

Definition and Management of Credit Risk

Before progressing further it would be appropriate to define what is meant by 'credit risk'. Credit risk is the measure of possible loss arising to the institution by the failure of any third party to meet its obligations as they fall due. Credit risk management therefore over the totality of a bank's business is of critical importance. An objective of a bank's management should be to so organise the total portfolio of credit risk that the failure of any individual third party, or group of third parties, should not seriously impair the bank's capital base, profit performance or cash flow.

There would appear to be four stages in the *management* of risk:—

— *identify* the areas where risk can arise; credit risk will be seen to arise in other than just the obvious areas of loans and advances to customers.

— *measure* the degree of risk; this can range from assessing an individual customer risk to reviewing the risks inherent in a particular industry or sector of the economy and will also involve careful consideration of the purpose of any loan advance or the nature of the project to be financed.

— *agreement on the level of risk* to be undertaken; which calls for judgment in balancing risk and reward as well as determining prudent levels of total credit risk exposure by individual entity, industry, country or line of business activity.

— *management of the business* to the agreed level of risk; which calls for ensuring an appropriate credit sanctioning, control and monitoring structure in an organisation with decisions delegated in the most cost effective manner but within an overall policy framework to ensure attainment of planned performance.

Credit Limits

All banks establish credit limits for their customers. These can range from an individual personal loan decision, which may be taken by a junior officer, to a major project financing proposal with extended maturities and repayment complexities, which could call for review by a number of senior executives in some form of credit committee. Whatever the scale of the credit decision, however, it is necessary for there to be the appropriate level of credit analysis so that risks can be identified and accurately measured. The setting of credit limits can be viewed as a restriction on business. It is preferable, however, to view limits as establishing a freedom to develop business within prudent parameters.

A total credit risk portfolio is an aggregate of many individual credit decisions. With the risk/reward patterns which prevail in many parts of the industry at present it can take just a few bad decisions to wipe out the profits on the remaining business. The best assurance of overall sound credit quality is, therefore, to ensure that disciplines and procedures are in place to prevent the unattractive risk from being undertaken at all, or at least to identify any signs of deterioration at a stage where corrective action is still possible. The individual credit decision may be taken with greater freedom and confidence if it is taken within an overall agreed policy framework for a particular category of business. A well constructed and well communicated credit risk policy will provide freedom for the business generators at the front line to seek and write business with speed of execution and confidence in the credit quality.

Current Influences on Risks in Banking

There can be little doubt that the banking industry – indeed the financial services industries as a whole – has been going through a period of considerable change in recent years and it is likely to be some while yet before this process decelerates. A number of aspects of change have naturally had an impact on the scale and on the awareness of credit risk. What is perhaps of greater significance is that all of these influences are occurring simultaneously.

It is during a period of rapid change that mistakes can be made. It is the responsibility of bank managements to ensure that change is managed in a constructive sense and that the validity of fundamental principles are not obscured. Elementary rules of lending which junior bank officers learn through their studies for The Chartered Institute of Bankers examinations and on internal training courses retain their validity when applied to more complex proposals and in spite of competing pressures. Basic rules include:

— knowing the customer, both personal qualities and qualities of management.

— judging the expediency of a proposal so that any exposure is in accordance with agreed bank policy regarding risk concentration or nature of business activity .

— ensuring that the amount of lending is reasonable, taking into account the purpose of the advance and the personal stake of the proprietor.

— obtaining satisfaction as to the source of repayment.

— not lending against security, but making sure that security where taken is properly appraised and perfected.

— matching remuneration to the degree of risk undertaken.

Such rules as these when summarised in this fashion may appear simple, not to say simplistic, but they are ignored only at the peril of the lending banker. I would submit that the principles of credit risk assessment and management have not altered significantly, although we are now benefiting from improved techniques and heightened perceptions of the risk management process.

A number of current influences which are impacting upon risks in banking are set out below.

Regulatory and Supervisory Changes

The regulatory and supervisory changes which have been introduced in the UK should be regarded by bank managements as supportive of sound credit management standards – and in broad measure I believe that this is the attitude which most would adopt. The 1987 Banking Act, which was preceded by a number of discussion papers, did not really introduce any fundamental changes in the manner in which credit risk is assessed and controlled.

The introduction of formal controls on large exposure risk concentrations largely reflected the sort of standards which bank managements were already observing. As for the co-ordinated proposals for the convergence of capital adequacy requirements which have been put forward by the Basle Committee of Supervisors these may also be seen in a positive fashion. The stated objective of attaining level playing fields for capital requirements for all banks operating in the world's main financial centres will reduce the capacity for the unhealthy aspects of competition and equally will reinforce the stability of the international banking environment by encouraging the observance of prudent levels of capital.

It is significant that the capital adequacy proposals are based upon the perceived credit risk in categories of assets. The risk ladder of assets – with credit risk equivalent weightings being decided by categories of product and also, in certain cases, by category of counterparty and by overall maturity – is a concept with which we are already familiar in the UK. Although it is always possible to discuss fine points of detail, the credit risk weightings applied to the various categories of asset would appear to coincide with the views of many banks.

Volatility of External Factors

Interest rates and foreign exchange rates have been subject to a very much greater incidence of fluctuation than in the years prior to the breakdown of the Bretton Woods 'fixed' exchange rate regime. This has naturally presented a challenge to corporate treasurers, particularly those working in competitive export markets on very fine margins. An unanticipated movement in exchange markets can quickly turn a major contract from profit into a loss, or indeed impact dramatically upon the very viability of the business itself.

There is now probably much greater general awareness of the significance of interest rate and exchange rate fluctuations than in the mid 1970s, when there were quite frequent examples of UK companies taking loans denominated in Swiss Francs and Deutschemarks, because they were attracted to the very low rates of interest compared with sterling financing, only to learn subsequently that any short-term advantage was more than offset by the exchange rate adjustment to the principal amount. There has also been an enormous growth in hedging instruments provided by banks to offset possible or unanticipated rate fluctuations. The development of financial engineering departments within the treasury operations of our banks is testimony to the ingenuity and resilience of the banking industry to cope with change and to develop new areas of business.

Management of interest rate and exchange rate fluctuations is of course every bit as important for the bank treasurer as it is for the corporate treasurer. Indeed banks have traditionally been organisations which are peculiarly sensitive to interest rate movements as they tend to be transformers of shorter term deposit liabilities into longer term assets. The new hedging instruments have therefore assisted these banks themselves in managing their own risks. Liability management has been recognised at senior management levels as requiring a degree of executive overview similar to the more traditional attention paid to the direction of the asset side of the balance sheet.

Market and position risk is of major importance in the provision of treasury hedging instruments. It is necessary for senior management to ensure that the writing or 'selling' of market risk positions is adequately covered by hedging models and/or is taken within carefully measured risk position limits. As well as market risk there is also, of course, credit risk involved in providing the tribe of products which has been fathered by the core range of interest rate and exchange rate swap and option instruments.

Off-Balance Sheet Credit Risk
The central bank supervisors have quite correctly taken steps to ensure that these off-balance sheet credit risks should be brought into the balance sheet for capital adequacy purposes. The credit risk can frequently represent quite modest amounts of the nominal principal amount of a transaction because what is being measured is the capacity of rates to fluctuate and the pricing implication for the replacement of an individual transaction in the light of this assessment. For example it might be determined that the potential for credit risk loss on a 12 month interest rate swap might represent no more than say 3% of the nominal amount of the transaction. It is important however for this risk to be understood, measured and controlled. In this connection it is perhaps appropriate to underline that the credit risk equivalent factors which have been put forward by the Basle Committee of Banking Supervisors for a range of off-balance sheet products are broad portfolio measures for capital adequacy purposes. The credit risk measurements for exposures to individual customers will normally be somewhat greater. A further very important measurement of credit risk which must be understood and controlled by bank management is the moment of delivery or settlement, particularly of course for those products requiring delivery of principal amounts, when the credit risk can be 100% of the nominal amount of the transaction.

The impact of external factors on risks and risk taking were highlighted by the October 1987 fall in securities markets. The pressures building up to such a dramatic degree of market adjustment are capable of some analysis – easier with hindsight than before the event – in a way that the oil price shocks of the 1970s were largely unpredictable. Events such as these can provide salutary reminders – if they are required – that bull markets do not carry on forever. One of the difficulties in assessing markets, particularly quite new markets such as those which have been developed for commercial paper and bank securitised debt, is the real depth of a market to cope with large and sudden movements. As a broad generalisation it can be asserted that we live in times of greater actual and potential volatility of external factors and these serve to heighten credit risk. However robust a hedging strategy a bank may have in place it is also important to have a well analysed and well understood structure for the control of credit risks flowing from it.

Competitive Pressures

Competition in the banking industry, like Topsy, always seems to be growing. It has to be acknowledged that competition is a "Good Thing" – as it encourages the delivery to the consumer of the best products at the lowest price and also rewards the most efficient producer. Competition between financial institutions does however have credit risk implications which bank managements need to keep in balance.

London has been a very open banking market for many years and our major corporate customers may at times feel that they have too many banks plying them with their wares rather than the reverse. One effect of this competition has undoubtedly been to drive profit margins to frequently wafer thin levels. The increasing pressures to gain and secure business from the prestige global corporates has been accompanied by the trend towards the issue of securitised paper rather than direct borrowing from the banks. The market in multi-option facilities has been expanding rapidly. An important credit risk issue for the banks, which has been flagged frequently by banking supervisors, is that as better assets are 'securitised' this could imply some dilution of the credit quality of the remaining portfolio. Equally important is the separation of the liability *commitment* to provide finance from the retention of the asset on the balance sheet. This form of standby commitment could mean that banks would be faced with making funds available just at the moment when market circumstances generally were least propitious.

Increased competition has been accompanied by a reduction in customer loyalty, both in the corporate and in the personal customer markets. It is only natural for customers to shop around for the finest terms from institutions frequently targeting on particular niche markets. There are dangers, however, in split banking arrangements if this obscures the flow of mutual understanding which can provide the confidence for longer term relationships through bad times as well as good. Even major corporates can benefit from some stability of core banking ties as a platform for sound business development.

Competition has been particularly marked in recent years in the personal customer market. There has been competition between banks and also from the new challenges presented by building societies, other financial institutions and major retailers. This competition is likely to gather momentum in all areas as the retail market continues to offer attractive prospects, particularly for institutions which can target key business areas without the cost burden of maintaining a range of financial services through extensive branch network delivery points.

There are, therefore, aspects of the competitive environment which impact directly or indirectly on risk issues. Banks collectively and individually have demonstrated that they are quite prepared to face competition. Bank managements will, however, need to ensure that the drive for market share does not simply lead to gaining the higher risk business at the margin. It is also appropriate to question the need to obtain marginally profitable business in one area of a customer relationship in order to profit or gain more remunerative business elsewhere. All of this demands adequate management information flows on which to take informed decisions. Banks have in the past been accused, with some justification of reacting to market competition with almost herd-like instincts. There have also however been increasing numbers of individual banks making considered withdrawals from markets where the balance of risks and rewards, particularly over a shorter time scale, was seen to be uninviting.

Technological Developments

Another major influence on the whole process of the identification, measurement and management of risk are developments in the field of information technology. Technology has been identified as one of the key factors – if not the key factor – in determining competitive advantages between different businesses. Developments in information technology are permitting radical revisions to the costs of developing and delivering new banking products and services – and productivity is clearly going to be a major battle ground for the financial services industry for the years ahead. The entry costs for new competitors to many areas of banking services will be drastically lowered.

The analysis and management of risk is based upon the processing of information. Indeed, banks – and financial institutions generally – have always been intensive users and transformers of information. The power of technology is now altering the structure of this process. New products are being developed, such as electronic payments systems and cash management, as a direct result of the new technology. At the same time new credit risks are being identified and measured in a new way: such as the settlement risk that can arise from the delivery of electronic payments systems.

Information technology will determine the key competitive factor of the cost of product delivery. It is also leading to a new understanding of business portfolios and to new avenues, such as those associated with portfolio management, for taking decisions on business risk. It is as if we are stepping from a two dimensional static black and white snapshot of risk portfolios to a moving three dimensional living colour representation. There has to be the closest dialogue between risk managers and those working in the specialist fields of information technology to ensure that strategic thrusts for the future will optimise the opportunities which are being presented.

Credit Risk Issues in Domestic Banking

Consumer Lending

There have been large increases in lending to the personal sector in the United Kingdom in recent years. This has helped to sustain the consumer demand which has been a major growth factor in the economy. In the three years up to and including 1986 the total of outstanding consumer debt rose at an average annual rate of 17/18%. In 1987 the rate of increase was 20%, to reach a figure for debt outstanding of £36·8 billion. The banking sector share of consumer debt has remained fairly constant at a little under 80% of the total and this represented £28·8 billion at the end of 1987. Within the banking sector figure, the amounts outstanding on credit cards have been increasing at annual rates in excess of 20% per annum, although there was some deceleration in the rate of increase in 1987 when the amounts outstanding on bank credit card lending reached some £6 billion.

The greatest increases in personal sector debt have however been in the area of house purchase loans. Amounts outstanding for house purchase loans to UK residents have been increasing at a rate in the region of 20% per annum. At the end of 1984 the total of loans outstanding was £109 billion and this had risen to £184 billion by the end of 1987, with the banks accounting for some £36 billion of this figure – a market share of a little under 20% compared with one of 5% at the end of the 1970s.

There have naturally been questions raised on the extent to which trends such as these are sustainable and also whether they are entirely healthy. It has to be said that patterns of large increases in volume in any area of banking activity attract the attention of bank managements just as they do that of bank regulatory authorities. Within bank portfolios there is little evidence so far to suggest a build-up of any significant problems. It is appropriate, nevertheless, in the present climate to continue to monitor the overall quality of the consumer lending book with particular care.

Macro economic data can often present difficulties of interpretation. For example, concern over increasing volumes of consumer borrowing has frequently been coupled with comment on the decline in the personal sector savings ratio. On certain measures, the personal sector savings ratio can be shown to have fallen from 14% of personal disposable income seven years ago to a current level of only 5%. This measure, however, which is derived from figures produced by the Central Statistical Office on disposable income and expenditure, needs to be balanced with statistics drawn from the financial accounts, and with this qualification a strong case can be made that the savings ratio has not fallen very drastically. Certainly there has been an increase in personal sector debt to income ratios. In the latter half of the 1970s this was fairly constant, with outstanding personal sector debt amounting to just under one half of disposable income. Since the beginning of the eighties debt outstanding has progressively risen and was over 80% of annual disposable income at the end of 1987. The figure for consumer credit alone, excluding house mortgage, has grown from under 10% in 1933 to over 13% in 1987. These rates of increase could not of course continue indefinitely without at some stage creating problems. It is appropriate however to place UK figures in the context of those of the USA where the comparable debt : income figures at the end of 1987 were in excess of 16% for consumer credit, and 87% for all personal sector debt including house mortgages. The macro economic data gives us useful but not conclusive evidence on trends in credit *quality*. Actual default patterns in bank personal loan portfolios give the banker more direct warning signals and for the time being these cannot be said to be cause for particular disquiet. Bank managements will however wish to monitor developments very carefully.

Mortgage Lending

The significant rise in bank house mortgage lending has occurred at a time of accelerating house prices. House prices, particularly in South East England, have been inflated to values which have been looking increasingly vulnerable. In the first half of this year house prices had risen to a level in real terms above the previous peak year in 1973 whilst the ratios of house prices to disposable incomes were also pushing the figures last seen in the boom 1973 year. However, even allowing for some correction to these house price levels the credit quality of the banks' mortgage lending would appear to remain very sound. There is a high proportion of former owner occupiers with a substantial element of equity within bank portfolios and overall, therefore, the very increase in house prices which has been seen has underpinned the value of the underlying security cushion. Meanwhile the traditional reliability of mortgage debt servicing should not be impaired.

Credit Scoring

As for the non-mortgage consumer lending by banks, much of the growth has been in the higher quality segment of the market. The development of credit scoring techniques, which are now widely adopted as a basis for credit risk decisions, provide a sound statistical basis for maintaining credit quality in new business development. The advantages of credit scoring in large volume lending is the reduction in operating cost coupled with speed of decision taking and sound credit quality decisions. It is however critically important in developing credit scoring to have available the range of detail of statistical data to permit refinement of scoring factors to adjust to evolving circumstances.

Marketing

Concern has been expressed that credit can be marketed aggressively and apparently somewhat indiscriminately. Institutions which do not have the same breadth of customer information which is available to the major retail banks, and which may also be under great pressure to maintain business volumes, may be tempted to take on poor risk business at the outset and to price for it accordingly. Credit risk managers in banks however should, and I believe do, recognise a responsibility both for maintaining the quality of their earnings and for the social aspects of lending policies. Whilst it may be reasonable for a marketeer to argue for a reduction in the credit risk pass score, as the increased volume of business this permits would more than offset the inevitable incidence of higher bad debts, it is the responsibility of bank management to ensure that credit standards are not impaired and to discourage individuals from overextending themselves financially.

Bad Debts

It is not possible to undertake large volume consumer lending business without incurring some bad debts. The incidence of default in bank consumer lending portfolios remains, however, at quite modest levels. That is not to say that there are any grounds for complacency, and bank managements are undoubtedly tracking all default indicators with great care. When a borrower does encounter unforeseen difficulties then banks are always prepared to review circumstances in a sympathetic and constructive fashion. It can happen however that difficulties arise because an applicant for credit has been less than frank in providing information about his financial commitments.

There is a limit to the degree of investigation which banks as a matter of commercial practice can reasonably undertake. In this regard bank managements are certainly aware of the advantages of pooling credit information. A great deal of effort preceded the decision by the banks earlier this year to pool so called 'black information'. If progress in the past had not been swifter it was largely due to the requirement of banks to ensure that there should be no breaches of the principle of customer confidentiality, and full co-operation with the spirit as well as the letter of an individual's rights under the Data Protection Act.

Corporate Customers

The willingness to take on term lending is perhaps the greatest change, with regard to impact on credit risk, which has occurred in the corporate customer market compared with attitudes which prevailed as recently as the late 1960s. An extension in the maturity of the commitment increases risk because it extends the time frame during which unanticipated developments can have an adverse impact on the trading position of a customer.

In addition to the extension of the period of credit risk there has also been a widening of the range of services and products which the banking industry can offer to the corporate customer. These can vary from the multi-option facility which is a rapidly expanding area of business, to the provision of electronic banking products such as cash management and automated payments facilities. A further development has been that of securitisation, with major corporates seeking to raise funds through issues of commercial paper or marketable notes, albeit on occasion with some form of bank standby arrangement, rather than through direct borrowing from banks.

Recently the clearing banks have been reorganising the manner in which they service the large corporate market. Teams of managers and specialist support staff have been set up which are dedicated to the corporate sector. This is a positive development as it permits a

more focused approach in dealing with the increasingly sophisticated needs of the corporate market. It also encourages a better
understanding by the banker of a customer's business and of the
markets in which he operates. A better link can be established with
merchant banking or venture capital specialists and a more
informed promotion of financial hedging instruments such as swaps
and options.

Credit assessment techniques have been enhanced with a move
away from the traditional 'gone concern' view of balance sheets to a
more dynamic use of going concern ratios and cash flow analysis. In
all of this training is most important. Progress with The Chartered
Institute examinations should be an indispensable part of the young
banker's technical development. This can be assisted by in-house
training and, at all levels, credit analysis can be greatly supported by
the use of computer-based expert systems. There remains great
scope for more extensive use of computer modelling techniques for
reviewing business projects to the benefit of both banker and
customer.

While bad debt provisions from third world sovereign debt
lending have been a setback for some major UK clearing banks, the
bad debt experience from the domestic corporate sector appears to
have been generally quite satisfactory. It is important, however, for
banks to have in place a structured approach for the early
identification of potential credit problems. A formal loan categori-
sation procedure, similar to that adopted by banks in the United
States, is a useful analytical support. The process should however be
viewed as a dynamic, action-orientated one designed to correct areas
of weakness for the benefit of both customer and bank.

Most banks have what might be termed intensive care units for
dealing with the corporate accounts which are deemed in need of
fairly remedial action. A particular problem which banks have had
to deal with since the 1986 Insolvency Act is the very real possibility
that the good banker who takes special steps to protect an ailing
corporate might be deemed a "shadow director" and hence become
liable to a charge of wrongful trading. Although the moratorium
made available to administrators of companies in difficulties is a
valuable option, the legal framework for the banker has gained in
complexity and this will call for very careful monitoring.

Fortunately, there has been a downward trend in the number of receiverships and also in the size of company which has been getting into difficulty. However due note should be taken that we are currently operating in a fairly benign economic environment. The cautious banker looking to the future should consider the possibility of the impact of rapid upward adjustments to interest rates as a response to any build-up in inflationary pressure, whilst the unresolved issue of the US balance of payments deficit may yet lead to a recession in the major export markets.

Industry Risk

Banks have a long tradition of understanding and analysing individual customer risk, but there are less well-established pro-cedures for analysing industry credit risk. Certainly a satisfactory analysis of an individual company requires a wider understanding of the market in which it is operating and an ability to place its competitive position among its industry peers. Corporate bankers therefore need the support of guidelines and data to assist in identifying key factors affecting particular industries.

A more structured approach to the development of an overall credit risk strategy for particular industries is becoming more evident. The initial framework for such a strategy will be expert economic analysis which can review historical trends, examine the market background and identify factors which are critical in an industry's short- and medium-term prospects. This framework may then be complemented by contributions from in-house industry specialists. Many banks, for example, have specialist shipping and aerospace teams as it is felt that business development in these areas requires detailed industry knowledge. Following critical analysis of an industry and its prospects, overall business guidelines can then be developed to enable marketing to be focused in a structured fashion and within prudent credit risk parameters.

An example in UK domestic banking of an industry which has for many years typically been supported by specialist industry knowledge is that of agriculture. This is an industry which has many small business units but where production cycles are frequently long and often complex. Even a banker familiar with farming and the complexities of the law and practice of the industry will benefit from the expertise that the industry specialist can offer – and so can his customer. Assessment of land quality is a specialist science, and is important in understanding the viability of a proposition, as well as the value of the security.

Settlement and Delivery Risk

The development of electronic payment systems has led to the identification and measurement of a new category of credit risk –
that of the daylight overdraft. To a certain extent of course this risk has always existed in paper-based payment systems such as the Town Clearing – but there it is rather diffused and bankers rightly take comfort from the ability to put in place physical controls to cover particular situations in case of need. Automated payment systems however permit and require formal credit limits over the extent to which payments are made in anticipation of incoming cover.

The volume of electronic payments continues to rise steadily – the items cleared in CHAPS for example have risen from 5 million when the system was first introduced to well over 8 million at the end of 1987. In the United States the Federal Reserve Board have already initiated action to control and reduce the total volume of daylight overdraft that was occurring across the various electronic payment systems – particularly CHIPS. If volumes continue to increase in our own CHAPS system there may be a similar pressure to review total levels of daylight risk arising, but there would be little advantage if settlement were simply to be diverted from an efficient electronic system to the paper-based Town Clearing. An area of possible increase in credit risk which does merit close attention by the banking industry concerns plans for new computerised book entry transfer systems for settlement of trading in securities and financial instruments in the London market.

The very successful automation of the Central Gilts Office book entry transfer system at the beginning of 1987 was based upon the banks assuring or guaranteeing the settlement of sales and pur-chases of gilts. This full credit risk was of an unlimited nature, albeit on the basis that the settlement banks should have a legal charge over the securities being transferred. Whilst the banks accepted this framework, in view of the standing of the parties involved and in awareness of the Bank of England's overall monitoring of the market and its participants, it should not fall to the bank to automatically assume the burden of credit risk assurance in the settlement role for other book entry transfer systems. The credit risk burden that would be placed upon the banking system, particularly at periods of severe market disruption, would be onerous indeed.

CHAPS volumes seem set to continue to climb, to the detriment of Town Clearing volumes which appear to be on a longer-term declining trend. It is essential that daylight overdraft limits be set with the same discipline of credit risk analysis as conventional overnight exposure, as, although the risk is very transitory in nature, it is potentially for the full amount of the limit in the event of a customer default.

Product Credit Risk Assessment

Product credit risk assessment is an important aspect of the identification and measurement of risk in banking. The first measurement of risk is the potential for credit loss arising from the default of any individual counterparty or customer. For many products this is fairly evident. For example the potential for loss in an unsecured loan of £100 to an individual is 100% of the sum advanced. There are, however, a range of products and services – such as the newer interest rate and foreign exchange rate hedging instruments – where credit risk measurement is far less obvious.

For the newer treasury products the assessment of credit risk frequently involves measuring the potential for future volatility of interest rate or exchange rate fluctuations and hence the replacement cost at the then current market values of dishonoured contracts. This requires both objective analysis of historic patterns and the exercise of judgment in projecting future trends. What is important is to adopt clear and well understood standards so that those who are responsible for corporate relationships can set satisfactory credit risk limits.

A further aspect of product credit risk assessment concerns the measurement of actual and projected default experience arising from a particular product or line of activity. Bad debts are a critical component of total product cost and must therefore be assessed with great care, particularly in the launching of any new products. An objective assessment of default incidence will have an important influence on the pricing of a product and the overall marketing approach. In a business such as banking, where credit risk is a critical determinant of overall performance, actual and/or projected bad debt experience may be a main component of the strategic decision on entry to or withdrawal from a particular line of activity.

Management of Credit Risk in Domestic Banking

Once risk has been identified and measured it still requires to be managed. I should like to summarise some of the important issues connected with the management of credit risk in banking.

The Importance of the Credit Ethic
In banking it is essential for the natural business drive to promote new business to be kept within the bounds of a prudent framework of credit risk guidelines. A "business at all costs" mentality will rapidly prove to be just too costly as in banking it is only too easy to gain market share by taking on other people's poor quality loans. It is most important, therefore, for business development targets and measures of performance – whether for the individual or the organisation – to include assurances on maintaining credit quality standards.

A separate credit control function has been proved over many years to be a sound means of protecting credit quality. In the present, intensively competitive environment it has to be accepted that the large corporate customer will frequently have a strong bargaining position. It is necessary, therefore, for the corporate relationship manager to have the support of a detached credit control function to balance the pressure from the customer side.

The manner in which credit risk appreciation is reflected in the actual conduct of business at all levels might be termed the 'credit ethic'. It is one of the greatest hidden assets in any bank. It is supported by sound training, clear credit risk guidelines, experience and consensus standards promoted by management. Without a strong and independent credit control function it is difficult to maintain.

Role of Portfolio Management

The traditional control of credit risk has been exercised at the account level. Increasingly however, there is an awareness of the role of portfolio management in the direction of the total spread of business. It has long been second nature for banks to avoid the build-up of risk concentrations in their lending books. Banks however are not in the position where assets are in immediately marketable form such that instant decisions can be exercised on the total portfolio mix of business.

The power of the computer can be harnessed to achieve a better understanding of the total risk portfolio through analysis by 'cuts' through various groups of assets. Assets may be reviewed by product, by industry grouping, by geographical area and by administrative units such as area offices and even individual branches. Measures can be developed for credit quality, and information comparisons can be drawn by viewing the profile of one part of the book against another. The reasons for relative differences in performance can be examined and decisions taken on the adjustments required to realise greater potential income or to correct inferior credit quality areas.

Risk/Reward

The balancing of risk and reward is an essential part of the credit risk decision-taking process. If, as a result of portfolio analysis, a block of assets is producing less income for a comparable degree of risk to a similar block of assets elsewhere then corrective action is called for.

At the level of the individual credit decision it is also necessary to ensure that appropriate reward is being secured for the degree of risk being undertaken. A prudent credit controller will look very closely at any proposal which is offering a generous return for the apparent degree of credit risk involved.

Allocation of Resources

The proposals for the convergence of capital adequacy which have been promoted by the BIS supervisors, and in broad measure supported by the EEC, are based upon the credit risk equivalents calculated to arise from both on- and off-balance sheet assets. In reviewing the risk/reward balance of the risk asset portfolio it is therefore necessary to consider the return on the underlying capital requirement.

An adequate remuneration of capital can occur only after deduction of direct and overhead costs of delivery of a particular product and after deductions for bad debts. The identification of the underlying capital requirement for a particular category of risk asset will establish a standard for measuring the risk/reward credit decision. If the convergence of capital adequacy proposals are adopted then one area which will command attention is the manner in which undrawn commitments are being satisfactorily remunerated.

Information Technology

A consistent theme throughout this review of the identification, measurement and management of risk is the reliance upon information technology. As has been mentioned, information technology is promoting – and is permitting – great changes in the banking industry. The extent to which this is controlled by individual banks will be a key factor in determining their competitive position amongst peer organisations.

The quality of credit risk decision-taking – from the credit score to be applied to the individual personal loan to the portfolio guidelines to be set for broad categories of risk asset – will reflect the quality of management information which is made available. A major responsibility for bank managements is to ensure that their information technology planning and investment reflect the priority to be given to credit risk management issues.

Conclusion

This paper has intentionally concentrated on credit risk issues in domestic banking. Bank managers are, of course, more than simply credit analysts. They need to be business managers, managing resources and working within a wide framework of business performance indicators.

Credit risk management is however part of the very fabric of banking. Banks are not, as some would have it, risk avoiders. They are rather risk takers – but only after those risks have been satisfactorily identified and measured. In a discussion paper issued by the Basle Committee of Banking Supervisors in March 1986 it was stated that credit risk had traditionally been considered the most important risk for a commercial bank and that poor asset quality had probably been the cause of more bank failures than had exposure to liquidity or market risks. The observance and maintenance of a credit ethic throughout a banking organisation requires the deployment of personal skills and commitment. This requirement is made easier by the establishment of a well understood structure of credit policy guidelines and procedures and by a strong and independent credit control function.

There are new pressures upon our bankers in today's very competitive markets, but there are also new techniques for responding to those pressures. Information technology, as in other industries, will be critical in determining the competitive advantages in managing credit risk. The statement made by Len Mather, one of my predecessors both within Midland and as President of The Chartered Institute of Bankers, almost a generation ago, however, remains entirely valid today:

> "The art of banking is surely to know when to accept the risk. But first the able banker must be able to appreciate and assess that risk".

John Robins

John Robins joined the board of Willis Faber Plc in February 1984 as Director of Finance and Management Services. He is responsible for the Finance, Treasury, Secretariat and Systems Divisions of Willis Faber as well as being Chairman of the Services Division of their principal international broking subsidiary, Willis Faber & Dumas Ltd.

He was born in India in 1939 and educated at Winchester College. Following accountancy articles with Touche Ross and National Service in the Gurkhas, he began his business career in 1961 in the electronics industry as a management trainee in marketing.

His career in the electronics industry concluded in 1974 after becoming Managing Director of an electronics company he helped to found, when he took over as Chief Executive of Bally Group (UK) Ltd, the UK subsidiary of the Swiss multi-national shoe retailing, wholesale and manufacturing group.

He joined Fitch Lovell Plc as Group Financial Director in 1979 and during his 5 years at Fitch Lovell he was part of the team that successfully fought off an unwelcome bid approach following a long monopolies commission reference. During this time he was Chairman of the Group's non-food interests and the Agricultural Products Division.

John Robins is Chairman of The Association of Corporate Treasurers and a member of the 100 Group of Chartered Accountants.

John Robins

3. RISK IN INTERNATIONAL BANKING — A CORPORATE TREASURER'S VIEW

Contents   *Page*

"IT LOOKS LIKE OVERTIME FROM NOW TO 1992"

RISK IN INTERNATIONAL BANKING — A CORPORATE TREASURER'S VIEW

Has the risk/reward ratio permanently changed for the worse for wholesale bankers?

Do all treasurers and their companies recognise the risks they are now taking for the undoubted rewards they are achieving?

I would like to state my conclusions to the questions I have raised above right at the beginning of this paper. I believe the answer to the first question is yes and to the second question no. As a treasurer I do not find this to be an altogether happy state of affairs and I believe there needs to be a greater understanding by both bankers and treasurers of how we can redress this situation to the advantage of both. My remarks are particularly addressed to the situation in the United Kingdom.

How has this situation occurred?

Banking in the 1960s and 1970s

The requirements of the average commercial UK client in this period were satisfied by a very simple wholesale banking structure. The UK clearing bank provided the everyday operating banking needs of the client. Basic borrowing requirements were provided by the overdraft, and loan finance was available for medium-term borrowings. The UK clearing banks made significant profits on these accounts – the client had no real alternatives.

Merchant banks and stock brokers provided the corporate finance advice, specialist financing for acquisitions and project finance and kept the client in touch with the "Financial Market Place". Overseas, the UK client would have one, maybe two, overseas banks which were often correspondents of their main UK bank. Foreign exchange and interest rates were not a major issue to the boards of companies. Finance directors had an easy life as far as those two aspects of their job was concerned.

In the early 1970s, with increasing inflation and huge capital shifts, the world woke up to highly volatile foreign exchange and interest rates. At the same time the growth in the number of banks operating in the UK was rapid and they brought with them knowledge of new "Financial Products" and opportunities for companies to reduce their costs of financing.

The American banks were particularly aggressive and successful in showing the finance directors of the time how they could reduce costs and improve service. The six "money centre" banks targeted the UK "The Times 1000" companies with Libor-based lending, term loans with covenants, and project-based finance, developed for their North Sea lending, backed up by account officers with industry specialisation. At the same time as this was happening, companies were devoting more time to expanding overseas. Consequently the control of overseas cash flows became an important issue. The larger companies, recognising the opportunities for cost reductions and the need for professional and day-to-day foreign exchange management, rapidly segregated these operations from the every day activities of the finance function into "Treasury" operations. By the late 1970s the treasury department was seen to be a specific requirement in most of "The Times top 500" companies. In May 1979 the Association of Corporate Treasurers was formed in the UK. This association was initially seen to be "Anti Bank" as it provided a forum for those wishing to discuss how to reduce the costs of commercial banking — its real value to both bankers and treasurers alike has increasingly been recognised.

During the late 1970s and early 1980s the trends firmed. The reward for commercial banking was reducing rapidly. Companies moved from having one UK clearing bank and a merchant bank to "multi banking". Again among the top 500 companies one could well see the treasury department dealing with up to ten or even more banks for wholesale money market and foreign exchange operations, whereas ten years before that same company might have dealt with just one single UK bank. The relationship between the company and its bank became one less centred around the chairman, financial director and the local director and more one between the treasurer and various directors of specialised operations within that bank. The life cycle of new financial products was becoming shorter, with a consequent effect on their profitability.

One response by bankers to this increasing reduction in wholesale banking profitability was diversification. Both geographic and product diversification accelerated and some very substantial losses, with a few successes, have been the consequence. We have seen the effects of the geographic diversification of some of the UK banks. In the area of product diversification, banks went into mortgage lending, estate agencies and substantially into life insurance and other types of personal insurance.

During this same period, the UK Government became increasingly concerned about the long-term profitability of substantial sectors of the UK stock market and "Big Bang" was a consequence. Yet another series of diversification moves were put in train. There can be very few of the investments made by the banks into this sector which are currently making a return on the investment, quite apart from making a profit on the capital employed.

So we have rewards reducing sharply and risks increasing substantially.

The Political Pressure on Banks' Profitability.

Government attitudes towards banks have often been negative. Banks are not always seen as being the necessary provider of the capital to fuel profitable industrial and commercial growth and are sometimes seen as manipulators of large sums of money for their own ends. Banks have been subjected to political direction to lend to the less developed countries with horrific results.

It is interesting to note that recently the Managing Director of the IMF criticised commercial banks stating that "the efforts by debtor countries to follow sound economic policies are being imperilled by the failure of commercial banks to lend them more money". Whilst one can understand his comments at a macro level, one can fully appreciate the shudders that ran round the board rooms of many banks when they read of that speech, only months after several hundred million pounds of loans had been written off. Banks are being subjected to increasing regulation and the new requirements on capital ratios are going to put profitability under increasing pressure. There is, however, no doubt that "1992" could present a major opportunity for some of the banks, but again there will be increased regulation, more intervention, and the rewards will only be for the few. Many will inevitably not make sufficient profits to cover the increased costs of capital that they will be employing.

Changes to Commercial Clients in the 1980s.

Against this background of reducing profitability in commercial banking in the early 1980s we find that the trading profits of most companies were being squeezed. The treasury function was seen as able to make "profits", and there were some companies which set up treasury departments as "profit centres".

Often the question as to what a profit centre is, is a matter of semantics, but in some cases, certainly, capital has been raised and lent to the treasury department for them to maximise profitability, sometimes with disastrous results. There was one large insurance broker, in early 1984, which had to write off over $100 million through losses in their treasury department. How many of the directors of that company really appreciated the risks that were being taken?

Foreign exchange is increasingly important to the boards of most companies through increasing multinational trade and the growth in overseas investments. The huge year-on-year swings seen in the foreign exchange markets mean that the currency effect on the profitability of companies has become a recognised issue in stock markets and the function of treasurers has been highlighted. The risks to companies in this area were highlighted by the "Volkswagen affair", which has cost that company DM480 million apparently as a result of fraudulent activities by one of their currency traders. Unfortunately the supply of good treasurers has not kept pace with the demand. The supply of treasury products has increased rapidly as banks have tried to increase their profitability. In some cases it is clear that the boards of companies are unaware of these new concepts and the risks that are being taken — as in the cases noted above. Could there be some banking boards who are also in this position? Has the pace of "new product" generation been too fast for careful consideration of the risks involved?

Sadly bankers and treasurers are increasingly seeing themselves on "opposite sides". Relationships have been under severe strain and the question is often asked by bankers "is relationship banking dead"? In the last few years we have seen a boom in takeovers, which of course have presented an opportunity for those who have provided the finance to make profits. Unfortunately there have been well publicised incidents where banks have soured rela tionships with their clients by being involved on both sides of takeovers.

One American bank has found itself under massive attack for its role in making the recent Beazer bid possible. The row became public in a big way just before Easter 1988, when a letter sent to the bank by the treasurer of the State of Pennsylvania was reproduced in a full-page advertisement in the New York Times. The tide of opinion is starting to run strongly against the transactions-led activities of some banks. In the UK in the last three or four years we have also had well publicised examples where bankers have pro-vided finance to companies making bids for their clients. The City of London has often been accused of "short termism". Pension fund trustees on one hand are requiring increasing returns from their advisors and yet have complained bitterly when those same advisors take profits during a bid for their own company! Is the same true here? Have treasurers so forced down the margins to the bankers that they cannot reasonably expect the same "relationships"?

The Market Place in the 1980s.

There is clear over-capacity in the wholesale financial industry. This is good news for treasurers, and bad news for bankers. Indeed part of the reason for the over-capacity is that an increasing number of treasurers are acting more and more like bankers.

A number of companies have set up extended financing opera-tions which are banks in all but name. We are not yet in the situation which exists in the US where paper issued by a number of corporates is at a higher credit rating than that issued by banks. The different regulatory practices in the UK rule out such a development on a large scale, at least in the domestic market. But we may well find companies, whose financing operations are particularly well run and well managed, discovering that they are contributing an increasing proportion of the group's total "profits". At some stage the regulatory authorities will have to decide precisely how to control this new risk in their market place.

The traditional advantage for bankers of their superior information compared to the corporate treasurers has been rapidly eroded, principally by the increasing number and declining costs of technology. Another factor has been the reduction in the cost of entry into the wholesale financial services industry.

As the treasury function becomes more specialised the willingness of treasurers to extend the numbers of financial institutions with which they deal has facilitated new entrants. I referred earlier on to the fact that the product life cycle of new financial products is becoming shorter and shorter. One reason for this is that some unthinking treasurers themselves are spreading the knowledge that they have about these new products in a way which will ensure that bankers do not return to them with new ideas in the future. The scope for truly valuable innovations (as opposed to gimmicks) is probably now very limited.

In general wholesale banking has become a "commodity market" and as such offers enormous potential scale but tiny margins. The successful are likely, therefore, to be those with good access to cheap funds as in Japan and the strong organisation, for example, of the Japanese and European Banks. Scope for generalist American banks to succeed in this environment would appear to be limited. I believe that the slope of the reward curve to treasurers has probably peaked and bankers are now increasingly turning their attention to retail financial services. The profitability potential there, for the short to medium term, appears to be radically different. The dramatic growth in demand for financial services is likely to continue for some time in the retail area. There is a parallel with the wholesale sector in that various services of banks are increasingly being segmented with competitors emerging within each segment. Technology has a somewhat subtle influence in this area. Where it reduces costs, banks clearly benefit. Where it facilitates new entrants or competitors to move into traditional banking areas, clearly the effects are opposite.

New forms of money transfer also offer great opportunities for banks. The old cheque clearing system would appear to be a major overhead for the clearing banks and treasurers may face a problem in this area shortly, with their costs rising rapidly. The building societies, free from this overhead, and with a strong branch network system and lower costs, pose a major threat to the banking industry in the UK. The societies are, nonetheless, not that experienced outside their traditional activities, and it remains to be seen whether they will stub their toes. I also believe that the building societies face increasing problems in some of the treasury products in which they are getting involved. The treasury function in the building society movement has, up to now, been totally focused on cash management. Entering into foreign exchange and swaps is a new dimension for them, and I wonder again how many of the building society boards fully appreciate the risks into which they are now entering. It is notable that building societies have taken market share away from the clearing banks over the last 20 years or so in the deposit market, thus further reducing the profitability of the banks.

Both bankers and treasurers are going to need to make adequate profits from "1992". I do believe there are significant opportunities for the UK merchant and clearing banks to make profits in wholesale banking in Europe. Overall the treasury function in Europe is not as developed as in the UK and many of the financial products which are now freely available to the UK commercial sector are not fully used in Europe. The one concern for European bankers must be that Japanese bankers will see Europe as a substantial opportunity and again provide funds on a very low cost basis.

Conclusion.

Wholesale bankers probably had it too easy for too long. They operated in a somewhat protected and privileged industry where competition was weak. That has now changed dramatically. For the corporate treasurer this presents increased opportunities, yet it also increases the burden of the job. New players, new products and even more aggressive marketing by suppliers create more scope for profit for the treasurer. They also make for complicated decision-making and substantially increase the risks.

I believe that there is now a significant opportunity for bankers to improve their profitability with commercial clients. There is an increasing awareness among treasurers that the risk/reward equation for wholesale bankers has been pushed down too far and that there must be profit on both sides of the transaction. There is growing emphasis in companies on having professional and trained treasurers. In the UK the Association of Corporate Treasurers, in conjunction with The Chartered Institute of Bankers, has been providing an increasing flow of trained treasurers to the market.

I do not believe however, that the bankers have yet communicated properly the need for their reward or the risks which they and their clients are taking in an increasingly technologically based world. How many treasurers or financial directors appreciate the business development costs of the new treasury products? How many recognise the cost of regulation? How many recognise the value of the relationships in their home territory when the new "product" exposes a risk in a territory where they have just made an acquisition (1992?). The opportunities for fraud are increasing, the scale of the transactions is increasing and the speed with which money is moved around the world is increasing, thus compounding the potential problems. Overall the risks are increasing rapidly for both bankers and treasurers. Greater and more effective communications between bankers and their clients (both treasurers and their chief executives) will be to the advantage of both parties, reducing risks and increasing rewards.

Thomas E Krayenbuehl

Thomas E Krayenbuehl studied at the Universities of Geneva and Zurich and graduated as a Doctor of Law in 1961. He then began a career which has involved him in banking and financial control as well as management in the United States, Germany and Switzerland. He went as a consultant to the European Free Trade Association in 1977 to organise its Industrial Development Fund for Portugal, and from there he moved in 1979 to the Union Bank of Switzerland in Zurich, where he is now Senior Vice-President and Head of a main department with responsibility for country risks, governments, and financial institutions for North America, Latin America, Asia and Australia.

He is a board member of several banks in which UBS has a participation and is the Swiss member of the Steering Committee of the EFTA Industrial Development Fund for Portugal.

Dr Krayenbuehl is the author of the book "Country Risk, Assessment and Monitoring". The second edition was published in April 1988.

58

Thomas E Krayenbuehl

4. RISK IN INTERNATIONAL BANKING – A BANKER'S VIEW

Contents

OUR DEBT CRISIS MUST BE GIVING
THE IMF MANY A SLEEPLESS
AFTERNOON

RISK IN INTERNATIONAL BANKING – A BANKER'S VIEW

Introduction

"International banking" is a term widely used in today's financial services vocabulary. If we intend, however, to analyse and investigate the risks inherent in "international banking", it seems to me necessary that we define clearly what we understand by "international banking" as referred to in this paper. "International banking" may embrace both wholesale banking and retail banking. Commercial banking and investment banking may also fall under "international banking". The differentiation between wholesale and retail banking is a distinction applied to customer segments. Wholesale banking, sometimes also called institutional banking, obtains its return on assets through relatively big transactions involving a limited number of customers, whereas retail banking, which provides services to the man in the street through relatively small transactions, needs a high volume to obtain the necessary return. Distinguishing commercial from investment banking has its origins in product orientation. I mention investment banking as part of "international banking" in addition to commercial banking because traditionally banks in many countries have in the past not been able or willing to engage in investment banking. It is therefore appropriate to make a distinction between these two types of "international banking". Like commercial banking, however, investment banking also delivers its products to the wholesale customer group and is, therefore, part of wholesale banking. Today nearly all larger banks are involved in commercial and investment banking in one way or another. I will, therefore, no longer distinguish between investment banking and commercial banking as separate types of "international banking", but only talk about wholesale banking.

I further intend to restrict the qualification "international" to banking transactions with specific characteristics. Within the scope of this paper I shall limit "international banking" to cross-border banking transactions. "International banking" is, therefore, basically wholesale, cross-border banking. It is of no significance whether a bank acts as a principal in a transaction or only as an arranger, since both types of activity can lead to an "international banking" transaction. I also include all banking transactions in which at least one party uses a currency that is not its home currency. The decisive factors for qualifying a transaction as an "international banking" transaction are the location of the different partners involved as well as the currency basis of the parties to the transaction. These two factors are at the root of the risks typical of "international banking". In this sense the so-called Euromarket is one of the largest single markets for "international banking" because a Euromarket transaction is a transaction where the borrower takes up a loan or effects a capital market transaction in a financial centre in a currency other than the one used for domestic transactions in that financial centre. Other important markets for "international banking" are the foreign exchange market, where billions of currency units are traded daily against other currency units, and the securities market, where millions of different securities change hands every day. Beside these markets, the traditional cross-border transaction to help international trade represents another important segment of "international banking". The tremendous performance of the Euromarkets and the foreign exchange and securities markets, coupled with the development of international trade, have made "international banking" an increasingly important factor for banking in general.

Major banks have taken the lead in this development and other banks have actively followed "international banking" trends by opening branches and subsidiaries in the major financial centres and time zones (table 1).

Foreign banking subsidiaries and branches

Table 1

	London	New York	Tokyo
1970	163	75	18
1975	263	127	52
1980	353	253	60
1985	399	356	74
1988	504	453	81

Source: The Banker and others.

"International banking" has become in many instances as important as domestic banking. This is shown by the comparison of domestic to international foreign assets of some of the largest banks worldwide (table 2).

Comparison of domestic with international assets

Table 2

	Domestic	International
Citicorp	57	43
Credit Lyonnais	47	53
Hong Kong and Shanghai Banking Corporation	25	75
Midland Bank	44	56
Royal Bank of Canada	69	31
Union Bank of Switzerland	47	53

Source: Annual Reports

However, as foreign branches of banks are often also involved in domestic banking in the countries they are located in, they do not operate exclusively in the field of "international banking". They provide services to customers in that market and I refer to this development as "banking internationally", not "international banking", because neither cross-border nor cross-currency transactions form the basis of such business. This has to be taken into account when looking at table 2. Let us now return to "international banking" and try to establish the catalogue of risks that are specific to this sector.

There are two major risk categories encountered in "international banking", namely, country risks and market risks.

Country Risks

In my book "Country Risk, Assessment and Monitoring" I described and analysed in detail all aspects of country risk exposure. I, therefore, limit myself here to a general overview of the topic.

Evolution

The country risk factor suddenly became a reality in 1982, when within a six month period, nearly all Latin American nations asked for part of their debts to be rescheduled and refinanced. While debtors in these countries continued to service their debts in local currencies, they were unable to obtain the necessary foreign exchange because their currency reserves were depleted and they were unable to borrow on the market the funds necessary to replenish them as their creditworthiness was suddenly impaired.

Definition

Country risks can be defined in the broadest sense of the term as the risks of incurring potential financial losses due to problems arising from macro economic and/or political events in a country (J. Calverley, Country Risks Analysis). This broad definition can be substantiated further as I have done in my book on country risks. My definition is:

> "Country risk is the possibility that a sovereign state or sovereign borrowers of a particular country may be unable or unwilling, and other borrowers unable, to fulfil their obligations towards a foreign lender and/or investor for reasons beyond the usual risks which arise in relation to all lending and investments. Country risk is composed of political and transfer risk."

Political and transfer risks are the two specific types of risk that have to be evaluated in order to reach a conclusion on the intensity of the risks of a particular country. The term political risk can be defined as the willingness to fulfil one's obligations, whereas the expression transfer risk is more concerned with the *ability* to fulfil one's obligations.

Assessment of Country Risks

As country risks are composed of political and transfer risks, the assessment of country risks has to take both aspects into account. While for the assessment of transfer risks we can rely on analyses of economic parameters, the assessment of political risks is much more susceptible to subjective opinions. The aim of country risk assessment should be to define the framework within which we can locate as clearly as possible the intensity of the risks. It is, therefore, advisable to investigate in some more detail the relationship between transfer and political risks and to find out how the two correlate. To my knowledge no academic research work has as yet been carried out on that subject.

We must therefore refer both to known events which indicate that there is a direct relationship between the two risk types in many instances, and also to events showing that political risks, in particular, can manifest themselves independently from transfer risks. It seems that increasing transfer risks very often entail a worsening of political risks. One such recent event was the limitation of servicing foreign debt to ten per cent of export earnings by Peru. The declaration by President A. Garcia was clearly a political act as he felt that it was politically unacceptable to sacrifice domestic economic growth by servicing foreign debt. The fact that Peru already at that time had difficulties in servicing its foreign debt is of interest but irrelevant in that context. However, one can still question whether the problems in servicing the foreign debt were not the cause of President A. Garcia's action. Another recent case is the declaration of a moratorium by Brazil on its medium-term debt in 1987. In this case it was also a political act, because Brazil would have been able to enter a rescheduling agreement and obtain a negotiated agreement instead of unilaterally declaring its intention to cease servicing its foreign debt. As is now evident, Brazil paid dearly for its decision. The refusal of the People's Republic of China to honour the debt of the Kuomintang Government was also a case of clear political risk. It is, in my opinion, essential to assess political and transfer risks independently before comparing them. How do we then best assess the two risk types?

The political risk or the will to honour one's debt should be assessed by analysing the political decision-making process of the country in question. In this context it is obviously of importance to locate the key players involved in that political decision-making process.

These key players may be political parties, individual persons, neighbouring countries, the church or economic and labour organisations, to name just some of the more obvious ones. The aim of political analysis is to discover how these key players interact and how they will influence the intensity of political risks in times to come. Political analysts are best suited for this purpose, but country experts can also be of help. The difficulty will always be to evaluate the intensity of the risks after the analysis. The use of weighted questions can give some additional guidance. While for bankers the intensity of political risks is in relation to the willingness to service foreign debt, investors see the political risk factor as residing in the government's attitude towards foreign investment as well as royalty and dividend remittance policies. The assessment exercise should be concluded by qualifying the political risks as high, medium or low, or somewhere in between.

Economic Indicators

The transfer risk or the ability to honour one's debt is easier to assess as economic indicators can be used. The indicators used should focus on the country's ability to earn foreign exchange, because it is foreign exchange that is needed to service foreign debt. The use of economic indicators can be supplemented by an analysis of the economic policies in that specific country, for example budgetary control, monetary policy etc. This analysis can be especially important when a country has to implement an adjustment programme because its economic indicators have deteriorated. Currently there is enough statistical material available to allow a fairly good assessment of the economic performance of most countries with the exception of some of the Comecon countries.

However, since the information deals mostly with the past, it is of limited use for the prediction of the future. At present there are no statistics available relating to the often crucial management of short-term foreign currency exposure over a useful time span. Of the different economic indicators used, the most common one is the debt service ratio. This ratio indicates the percentage of export earnings that is needed to cover the debt service, i.e. interest and amortisation on the medium- and long-term debt. A ratio of 25 per cent and higher can be considered as a situation which needs careful watching.

The International Institute of Finance in Washington, an organisation founded by major international banks, produces economic data which is very helpful for analysing a country's performance because it focuses on the needs of "international banking". The process of assessing transfer risks should result in a second classification of country risks according to intensity such as high, medium or low risk, or even on a more differentiated scale.

As economic indicators should give a fair view of a country's financial position, one could assume that similar parameters lead to a similar qualification. However, this is not always the case, as the examples in table 3 below show.

We are also faced with the phenomenon which I would like to call creditworthiness, namely the potential of a country to obtain funds internationally in all different financial instruments. The creditworthiness of a country is only partly determined by a careful assessment of country risks and is to some extent affected by the opinion-makers on the international capital markets.

Economic Indicators (all figures for 1987 and in US$M10 unless otherwise noted)

Table 3

	Total External Debt IIF Estimate	Total External Debt in % of GDP	Trade Balance	Current Account Balance	Interest Payments as % of Exports	Interest Payments as % of Foreign Exchange Earnings
New Zealand	27600***	81	−16	−1250	27·5	20·4
Ireland	27700	102	1800	−250	14·7*	12·7*
Canada	193500	46	3673	−7235	15·5**	13·2**
Brazil	117000	38	11150	−1900	37·4	33·4
Mexico	104600	79	8300	3600	38·0	34·7*
Columbia	17100	48	400	−500	26·9	19·9

*   1986 Figures
**   1985 Figures
*** Official Estimate

Source: International Institute of Finance

Beside the individual country risk assessment, one can also use the ratings that are established by several companies and institutions at regular intervals as guidance. The best known are the International Country Risk Guide, the BERI Index and the ratings published by the Institutional Investor and Euromoney. These ratings are, however, of a general nature and do not help to solve specific needs. They are nevertheless helpful for checking one's own conclusions.

After having made an assessment of the political and transfer risks, one obtains for each of these risk types a qualification of its intensity. How these two risk factors correlate is not known exactly.

Therefore, in order to judge country risks properly, one has to see if the two risk types differ very much in intensity. If this is the case, the assessor has to establish which of the two risk factors is more important and place more emphasis on that aspect of the country risk exposure.

Monitoring Country Risks

In order to control country risks, it is important to establish a monitoring system. The assessment system gives us the relative intensity of country risks at a specific moment in time. Through a regular assessment at well defined time intervals one can observe the development in country risk intensity which can then lead to respective changes in business policy. In order to limit country risk exposure further, it is advisable to establish country limits for each country with which one engages in international banking.

In addition, a break-down of the country limit according to type of business and tenor adds fine tuning to the monitoring of country risk exposure. The size of the different country limits, as well as the actual exposure, should be in line with the risk absorption potential of the bank involved. Country risk exposure has also become a concern for banking supervisory authorities which in all major countries have undertaken steps to guide banks. Industrial companies or investors with cross-border exposure have to adapt the country limit concept according to their own needs.

Reducing Excessive Country Risks

As I said before, country risk exposure has made many banks uneasy about international banking. When going over their country risk exposure "books", these banks felt that they had lent too much to certain countries and, therefore, thought about ways of reducing their excessive risks. They were inclined to do this because, in most rescheduling agreements over the past few years, they were asked to put up fresh money amounting to three to eight per cent of their current exposure, thereby increasing their exposure even further. A secondary market for the trading of rescheduled debt has therefore developed. This market is dominated by relatively few houses and is a negotiated market. Over the past few years, the values of the secondary market have continually declined, as shown in table 4.

Secondary Market Prices for Developing Country Debt (Percentage of Face)

Table 4

Country	Jul 85	Jan 86	Jun 86	Dec 86	Jun 87	Dec 87	June88
Argentina	60–65	62–66	63–67	62–66	57·5–58·5	30–31	24–25
Brazil	75–81	75–81	73–76	74–77	61–63	45–47	50–51
Chile	65–69	65–69	64–67	65–68	68–70	62–63	60–61
Colombia	81–83	82–84	80–82	–	85–88	65	65–66
Ecuador	65–70	68–71	63–66	63–65	51–54	35–36	25–26
Mexico	80–82	69–73	55–59	54–57	57–59	51–52	50–51
Peru	45–50	25–30	17–23	16–19	14–17	8	6–7
Philippines	–	–	–	72–76	69·5–72	50–51	53–54
Poland	55–60	50–53	43–46	41–43·5	43–45	42·5–43·5	41–42
Romania	85–89	91–94	89–92	86–89	86–89	82–83	86–88
Venezuela	81–83	80–82	75–78	72–74	71–73	55–56	54–55
Yugoslavia	74–77	78–81	77–79	77–81	75–77	48–49	45–46

Source: Shearson Lehman Bros. Inc.

The heavily indebted nations have taken steps and also introduced special schemes to diminish their own debt in order to reduce their debt servicing burden. The most widely accepted systems are the debt to equity conversion programmes which vary, however, from country to country. In this connection one can also mention the Mexican bond issue at the beginning of this year which was backed by US treasury bills with a zero coupon, or the exit bond schemes introduced by some countries. The reduction of excessive country risks has become possible, but it is a lengthy process and usually involves a substantial write-down for the banks involved.

Market Risks

The other major category of risks to look at in "international banking" are the risks connected with market fluctuations. The market risks we are talking about are those associated with the foreign exchange, interest and securities markets. Constant changes in the development of foreign currencies and interest rates create further substantial risks in "international banking". These risks are often also on the liability side of a bank's balance sheet and have, therefore, to be dealt with by the treasury department. Banks have handled market or price risks of foreign exchange transactions mostly through risk-offsetting transactions or matched positions.

As offsetting transactions not only reduce the risks but also the earnings potential, banks allow their traders or dealers open positions within clearly defined limits. The risks involved in these open positions should be well within the risk absorption potential of the banks involved and demand careful monitoring by the top management of the bank. Due to the development of the so-called newer products, banks have several different possibilities open to them to hedge their risks.

If we look at a foreign exchange forward transaction, such as buying from a customer US dollars against delivery of Deutschmarks in six months, the bank can try to offset the transaction risk through an exactly matching transaction with another customer. The bank can also hedge the transaction in its own books by selling the US dollars against Deutschmark spot, taking up the US dollars and placing the Deutschmarks on the market. A third possibility could be to hedge through the currency option market by arranging the buying of a Deutschmark option on a call basis so that the buyer of the Deutschmark knows the price when the transaction is concluded. The bank can either arrange the option for its customer or write the option itself. In the latter case, the bank has to face the additional risks associated with writing options. I do not intend to talk about the risks of writing options in this paper because the subject would be too vast. A fourth but very risky possibility could be just to make the transaction without hedging it and running open positions for the respective amounts. This very short description of how a bank can handle the risks involved in a forward foreign exchange transaction shows that in view of the different possibilities some ingenuity is required if a bank is to face the risks of such a transaction and at the same time optimise the risk reward relationship.

The problem of interest rate sensitivity is as much present in international banking as it is in domestic banking. The mismatching of the tenor of assets and liabilities has always been a problem for banks but has also provided them with opportunities. Traditionally the interest yield curve is such that profitability is enhanced for banks by borrowing on a shorter tenor than lending out. However, there has been much more than one occasion when the market moved to a negative yield curve and medium-term lending had to be supported with expensive short-term funds. The inherent market risk and the risk of interest rate development on foreign currency transactions are often coupled with liquidity risks because the last resort lender cannot provide the necessary liquidity to foreign banks.

On the interest side we also find product developments that enable banks to hedge their risks as well as lower their borrowing costs. The medium-term interest rate swap or interest rate and currency swaps are examples of such price risk transferring innovations. The forward rate agreement (FRA) is another such mechanism through which the buyer can protect himself against a rise in interest rates, whereas the seller protects himself against a decline in interest rates. The FRA is, therefore, a somewhat more tailor-made interest future contract. Another interest protection instrument is the interest option. To offset interest movements different hedging techniques are available offering protection and banks have to choose those that are most adequate for their funding requirements.

Further market or price risks are to be encountered on the capital markets and in the securities industry. I will only deal with the ones of the primary capital market because these are normally not hedged. Market risks in the trading of securities are also similar to those in the trading of foreign exchange and can be hedged in a similar way. The risks the primary market entails are attributable to the time lapse between the pricing of an issue and the closing of an issue, i.e. market conditions or a change in perception. This is especially true in an unstable interest rate environment, whereas in periods of steady interest rates and trends the market risks are often due to the aggressive pricing of an issuing house. If the capital market transaction is equity linked, the developments of the respective stockmarkets create additional uncertainty. Some years ago the risks were smaller because capital market deals were priced after they had been organised and bought deals were unknown. International competition has brought not only tighter pricing but has also substantially increased the market risks for issuing houses.

Market risks are important risks in international banking. Hedging techniques are available for many market risks, but they have to be paid for, thereby lowering the profitability of the banking operation. In some areas, however, risks have to be borne directly by the banks involved, and consequently have to be covered by an adequate risk absorption potential.

Other Risks Involved in International Banking

Credit Risks

Credit risks in international banking are basically the same as in national or domestic banking. The prudent banker has to ask his borrowers the same questions and make the same investigations as in domestic banking. Questions like "How are you going to pay me back?" or "What are we going to do if your plans fail to work out?" are to be asked with the same insistence. There are sufficient techniques for evaluating credit risks available to analysts to enable them to make a reasonable estimate of the future by referring to past experiences. In the case of cross-border loans, analysts often have to base their work on accounting systems that are different from the ones at home. It may prove much more problematic to procure information about international credit operations than about domestic loans. Knowledge of the market in which the borrower operates, as well as knowledge and experience of the legal situation of a foreign country, make credit risk appraisal more difficult. Language and culture can play an important role in the relationship with a foreign client and, thus, in evaluating a credit risk. Apart from techniques of credit appraisal, additional knowledge has, therefore, to be promoted in banks engaged in cross-border lending. This supplementary knowledge is needed because it is not part of the natural know-how that domestic lending departments have acquired over years of lending. As the world changes ever more rapidly, the value of many techniques and previous know-how becomes quite limited.

The ability of a borrower to service his debt and the worth of his assets depend today much more on the plans for the future and the resultant cash flow that can be obtained than on his past performance. To obtain such knowledge, the borrower and the lender have to co-operate very closely. As this is normally more difficult in cross-border lending, banks tend to limit cross-border lending to credit risks of the highest standard, where it is assumed that, if the past has been managed well, the future also has a chance of being fairly trouble-free.

Another way of limiting risks in cross-border transactions is to concentrate on lending to state-owned borrowers or government agencies, i.e. so-called sovereign risks. This path is often chosen in non-industrialised countries. Such lending requires a careful analysis of the legal or contractual relationship between the borrowing entity and the respective national institution which controls the disbursement of government funds. In such cases the assessment of country risks will also be of the utmost importance.

In view of the difficulties entailed in assessing longer-term credit risks in international lending, some banks limit themselves to short-term commitments because they feel that in these cases a successful historical performance is enough assurance for the short-term commitment undertaken. These transactions are often also of a self-liquidating nature. The most common type of short-term credit risk is trade financing, be it import financing or pre-export financing. All spot and most forward foreign exchange transactions fall under this category.

The use of project financing techniques to limit credit risks is a more sophisticated approach. However, such a technique can only be applied if the borrowing unit is clearly defined and possesses a cash flow generating capability within the jurisdiction of the borrowing unit. Credit appraisal of these projects is made to analyse the costs of implementing them and to evaluate the probability of the assumed cash flow. A thorough credit appraisal often needs the assistance of outside consultancy with engineering, mining, marketing and construction experience. Simulation techniques can be used to evaluate the project under different assumptions. Leveraged buy-out financing is, in my view, another special type of project financing. In these cases the cash flow for the repayment of the loan often stems from the disposal of assets.

Credit risks in international banking tend, therefore, to be either sovereign or highly respected companies. Project financing techniques are also used for specific lending risks. Furthermore, one tries to limit the risk through the shortness of the term of credit. All these credit risks produce assets for the banks involved and are part of international banking if they are taken up through a cross-border transaction or involve foreign currency risks.

Banks that are active in the capital markets have to make similar considerations if they bring a borrower to the international capital market. In these cases the credit is securitised and sold to institutional and private investors. The quality of the credit risk has to live up to the highest standards because medium- or long-term commitment is normally involved.

Although the arranging bank is not directly responsible or liable for the credit risks, its standing as issuing house is obviously at stake. Credit risk failures in international capital markets transactions have, therefore, been very rare.

As a special case of credit risk I would like to mention here lending to holding companies or lending on the basis of a consolidated balance sheet. The establishment of a consolidated balance sheet as well as a profit and loss statement is of more interest to the investor, wishing to see the whole economic value of the company, than to the banker. The banker has to base his credit appraisal on the asset strength and earnings potential of the specific company he lends to in the knowledge that under extreme circumstances it might not be possible to move liquidity around to settle group liabilities even if tax and foreign exchange regulations would allow it. So far cross-border lending to holding companies has produced no casualties since these are often multinationals, usually well managed and always able to borrow in case of need on the strength of the group's name. As a last resort the holding company can always be broken up.

Banks have established a relatively good record on handling credit risks in international banking. This has been mainly due to the cautious approach adopted in selecting credit risks. It is, therefore, not so much the credit risks in "international banking" that have led to a certain uneasiness about it, but the country risks with which I have already dealt. Larger credit losses were only incurred when banks started to overlend to specific sectors such as shipping or real estate. Just as we have economic cycles that affect particular sectors of the national economy, comparable developments influence the global economy.

To monitor credit risks well in international banking, banks will have to continue to apply high standards of credit analysis and define clearly the segments in which they intend to market their products. These internal policies should ensure that no single credit risk can seriously damage the risk absorption potential of the bank in question. On the other hand, an above-average quality credit risk means substantial pressure on margins. Within the OECD countries "international banking" has, therefore, become highly competitive. Beside country risk problems, this aspect of international banking has probably also induced some of the major regional banks of the United States to pull out.

Settlement Risks

Another risk category now encountered much more frequently in international banking than previously is the so-called settlement risk. What are settlement risks? Settlement risks comprise all those risks that can arise after parties to a transaction have reached an agreement. While these risks had for many years been associated only with a specific transaction between counterparties, today they are also associated with the settlement procedures and mechanisms of certain banking products.

When we talk about settlement risks between two parties to a transaction, we mostly mean documentation risks. One can reduce these risks by clearly describing and fixing the terms on which the transaction is to be executed.

In international banking, lawyers have been called upon to establish correct and efficient documentation for most international banking products. As Anglo-Saxon law provides the basis for most of these transactions, the absence of a codified law has led to highly elaborate legal documentation. If new products are introduced in international banking, standard documentation is usually developed by the major law firms in a fairly short time span.

Another type of settlement risk is of a financial nature and involves the same counterparties who have to settle different transactions coming from the same or different products on the same day. These are the most common risks to be faced when financial institutions deal with each other. Typical examples are the foreign exchange spot transactions that the very active international banks do with each other every day. US dollar/Deutschmark transactions can run into hundreds of millions spread among dozens of transactions between two counterparties. To minimise the settlement risks, banks have developed netting systems whereby only the net amount due is actually transferred. To my knowledge such a system is employed by several banks on the London market. If banks deal with each other in many different products, the amounts to settle on a specific day may be very substantial, since we might have to add together payment orders, forex transactions and money market transactions. The need to establish specific settlement limits is often discussed and some banks have introduced them for each other.

These settlement limits are relatively easy to establish and control if we look at a specific account relationship, e.g. a Pound Sterling account of a Swiss bank with a British clearing bank. The situation becomes much more complicated if a large bank wants to control all the settlements which it has with another large bank since they deal in many different products with each other every day. Personally I question the viability of such an exercise and would much more recommend a careful choice of potential counterparties.

A third type of settlement risk is that associated with settlement systems. Settlement systems are basically domestic institutions, and have been mentioned by Mr John Brooks in his paper. International banking is concerned with the risks inherent in domestic clearing or settlement systems only inasmuch as it relies on those systems to settle transactions. This class of risk also includes exchange risks, whether stock, commodity or futures exchanges. Such risks became apparent when Hong Kong closed its stock exchange after the October 1987 crash. Furthermore, if we talk about securities trading we also have to take into account the risks that delivery incurs because paper has to be moved from one place to another. It is quite astonishing how archaic the security delivery systems are in many countries. Worldwide unification of securities delivery systems for which the same delivery and settlement time spans are prescribed for the corresponding money transaction is only one of the several changes necessary to diminish the delivery risks. A changeover to paperless securities would be another step in the direction of reducing such risks.

Settlement risks encompass a wide variety of risks, some of which are beyond the control of a bank. Through directives and by taking organisational steps, banks can minimise in-house settlement risks. Outside settlement and delivery risks can only be contained through the active cooperation of all parties involved as well as by the respective supervisory authorities. In most areas the respective supervisory authorities are well aware of the risks and manage them in a very appropriate way. As these systems also depend on sophisticated and large-scale computer technology, one has to realise that this may lead to risks that are difficult to foresee and, once present, certainly hard to keep under control. An example was the breakdown of the computer system of a New York bank participating in the CHIP system.

Product Risks

Many new banking products have been developed over the last ten years. These so called "newer banking products" have not yet established a risk record and, therefore, present the international banking community with new risks that are also difficult to evaluate. The central banks of the Group of Ten commissioned a study group to investigate some of these risks. The results of this investigation were published in the highly acclaimed book on "Recent Innovations in International Banking", published by the Bank for International Settlements, Basle, in April 1986. All of these new banking products such as note issuance facilities, medium-term interest and currency swaps, foreign currency and interest options as well as forward rate agreements – to name only the most widely used – involve a credit risk because there is always a counterparty.

In addition, there are some specific risks which are typical to one or other of these products. The note issuance facility also involves liquidity risks which are common to all contingent liabilities as long as the facility is not used. In contrast to other contingent liabilities, such as guarantees or confirmed letters of credit, the liquidity risks incurred in connection with note issuance facilities are, however, different since liquidity may become due at the very moment when international liquidity is also tight. As the liquidity which the bank has to provide in international banking is frequently not in its own currency, national liquidity provision schemes fail to work. Banks have, therefore, to establish policies on how they want to control the liquidity risk – that is, the funding risk inherent in this product. This can be done through back-up lines, long-term funding agreements and a limitation of commitments for these products. Medium-term swaps as well as foreign currency and interest options must contend with yet another additional risk factor, namely, price risks. As the market in these products has developed substantially, and exchanges offer standardised currency and interest options, banks tend to offset their price risks by entering a hedging transaction. This obviously reduces the income to the buy and sell spread but also limits the price risks. What, however, remains is a replacement risk if one party fails. This is also true for forward rate agreements, which are, in effect, an over-the-counter financial futures contract. Forward rate agreements are heavily used to manage interest risks or market risks better.

Some of the risks connected with the new banking products can thus often be neutralised by offsetting them against a countertransaction. This limits the profit potential though. Liquidity and replacement risks, however, as well as being unavoidable, are difficult to assess fully. They can be contained by means of appropriate guidelines and a consistent control of all the commitments taken and by comparing them with the risk absorption potential of the bank involved.

Conclusions

As we have seen, the risks involved in "international banking" are manifold. Some of the risks are similar or even identical to those encountered in domestic banking. Other risks are typical for "international banking". In order to control and manage successfully the risks of "international banking", banks have to acquire the necessary expertise to analyse and handle them. A cautious approach is especially recommended if an adequate diversification of the risks is not possible and hedging techniques are not available. Furthermore, monitoring systems should be established for all risks so that the current exposure is always known. In addition, the management of a bank should not forget that for each risk taken an adequate remuneration should be achieved. The pricing policy for products in "international banking" has to reflect this.

The weighting of the different risks undertaken and analysis of the corresponding remuneration will enable the bank's management to see if the risk absorption potential really justifies taking all these risks. The successful bank manager will always be aware of this.

CASE STUDY

THE GULF AGGREGATE PROJECT

Aspects of the relationship between international banks and their multinational customers – perceptions of risk – constraints imposed by regulators – responding to customer needs

Background
American Stone Inc. (AMSTONE) has extensive knowledge of the aggregate business, particularly in the South East and Mid-West USA. In the late 1960s, the company noted the few, if any, alternatives to existing sources of aggregate (i.e. locally from crushed stone, gravel deposits from dried up river beds and flood plains, and shell material dredged locally offshore) along the Gulf Coast region of the United States. These sources began to be exhausted in the mid 1970s as local quarries ran out and environmentalists began to exert pressure to put an end to local dredging. Supplies then had to be freighted in, sometimes from great distances. Prices began to rise and quality to fall.

The major markets along the Gulf Coast are Houston (approximately 43%), New Orleans (16%) and Tampa (32%).

Concept
By the late 1970s, AMSTONE saw the opportunity to provide an alternative source of aggregate. A project was established to:
1. Find a long-term source of high quality stone.
2. Find a source of stone close to deep water channels to minimise transportation costs.
3. Locate a reputable joint venture partner with knowledge of local business conditions.
4. Establish a reliable and low-cost means of transportation from source to the Gulf Coast.
5. Conduct extensive research on local market conditions along the Gulf Coast.
6. Select sites along the Gulf Coast for delivery of the aggregate.

An extensive search was conducted throughout those areas of the Caribbean, Mexico and Venezuela with limestone deposits. By the beginning of the 1980s, the Yucatan Peninsular in Mexico was selected as meeting the project guidelines and being close enough to the Gulf to keep transportation costs to a minimum.

Existing Mexican regulations strengthened the perceived need to have a local partner and Mexico Construction (MEXICON) was selected. A joint venture agreement was signed by 1982. Discussions then began in earnest to purchase the necessary land, set up the financing and framework of the joint venture companies, obtain necessary operating permits in Mexico, and conduct market studies in Houston, New Orleans and Tampa.

This work took five years and the three primary joint venture companies were established towards the end of 1987.

The Sponsors

American Stone Inc. (AMSTONE)

AMSTONE is the largest producer of aggregate (crushed stone of various sizes for housing and commercial construction, road construction, and concrete) and operates in excess of 100 quarries and gravel plants in the South East and Mid-Western areas of the United States.

It had 1986 sales of 100 million tons of aggregate. The following figures relate to the same period:

Net sales (including other interests)	– US$950m
Net earnings	– US$90m
Funds flow	– US$190m
Total assets	– US$840m
Net worth	– US$500m

Mexico Construction (MEXICON)

MEXICON was founded forty years ago and is the largest construction and engineering firm in Mexico. It has proven experience in heavy construction, dams, and harbours (including dredging).

Consolidated revenue for 1986 was US$600m with funds flow of US$95m and net worth at US$220m.

The senior and line management of both groups is strong and has the capability of dealing with a project of this magnitude and of pooling resources on a joint venture basis.

Project Organisation

For technical and regulatory reasons, and in order to define and separate the major risks, three companies will be formed – QUARIMEX, CARISTON and AGGREMEX. A brief description of the function of each company is set out below and Appendix 1 contains an organisation chart showing the relationship between the companies and indicating the level of financial requirements and the proposed sources. Appendix 2 shows the role of the joint venture companies in pictorial form.

Whilst it is necessary to have Mexican control over Quarimex, the weight of the management decisions on the project overall will fall to AMSTONE.

QUARIMEX

The company will quarry the rock, crush it, transport the aggregate produced to the local dock facilities and load the aggregate onto bulk carriers for transport to the United States.

It is organised as a Mexican national company in order to satisfy Mexican regulations and qualify for special treatment under Mexican tax laws.

Mexicon will nominate five board members and Amstone four. All major decisions of the board will require a majority of 75% of board members.

The major elements of Quarimex's operation are:

1. *Reserves*

   Following extensive tests, Amstone estimate reserves of 260 million tons or forty years' supply.

2. *Port Construction*

   Quarimex will construct the ports to take the two 60,000 DWT (dead weight ton) bulk carriers to be built by CARISTON. This will involve removing 250,000 cubic metres of limestone, which will form the initial aggregate supply source. The port facilities will be assigned to local (Mexican) government against a thirty year leaseback. Completion is scheduled for June 1988.

3. *Production*

Quarimex will begin to crush the limestone from the dredging operation in temporary plant constructed at the port site. Construction of permanent plant will commence at the same time and take two and a half years. The company will be able to produce the entire range of aggregate products required by the Gulf Coast market.

4. *Labour*

The company will be responsible for recruiting its own labour force under supervision of the major sponsors. No labour supply problems are expected.

5. The company will be responsible for constructing houses for the labour force and offices on site.

6. *Permits*

Regulatory approval for the project was required from three Mexican authorities – Urban Development and Ecology; Ministry of Communications and Transport; and the State Government. Permits to mine the rock, build the port and operate the quarry were issued in 1986. This was a lengthy process and extensive work had to be completed on the environmental impact of the project. The time, expense and effort required to obtain these permissions provide a major barrier to the entry of any competitive operator.

7. Quarimex will contract exclusive distribution rights to AGGREMEX and is under an obligation to supply all that the company can purchase. Sales to third parties will not be permitted until Quarimex has fulfilled its obligations to Aggremex.

CARISTON

The company will own two 60,000 DWT bulk carriers and will have long term use of a smaller ship of 35,000 DWT under a contract with Capital Steamship Line (CSL).

Recognising the considerable potential operating risk, Cariston has used a wide spectrum of specialist consultants to advise on the specific ship building contract, the design of the vessels, loading, affreightment, contracts etc. In addition, CSL has been contracted to manage the bulk carriers under a five-year management contract covering both operations and maintenance. Cariston is also aware of certain 'local content' requirements on US Federal projects, and CSL will arrange chartering of US flagged vessels should there be a need.

The major decisions taken by the company have been:

1. To purchase the ships rather than charter them.

2. To purchase new vessels rather than second-hand ships needing refurbishment and redesign.

3. The choice of the shipbuilder. Consideration was given to yards around the world, including Norway, Spain, the UK, Japan, Korea and Brazil. The final decision, backed strongly by CSL who already own three similar-sized bulk carriers out of the yard, was for a Brazilian company, 'Verolme'. The contract price was not the lowest offered, but was backed by a significant interest equalisation payment and commission provided under the Brazilian export programme. The payments are to the lending institution but are generally rebated to the borrower.

4. Supervision of the shipbuilding to be by CSL under a separate contract. (CSL has extensive knowledge of this type of construction contract).

5. Ship registration – in the Bahamas.

6. Operations and maintenance to be under the contract with CSL.

7. Insurance under CSL's umbrella policy.

8. Legal structure – principally the contract between Cariston and Aggremex, where Aggremex will be bound to use Cariston ships to their capacity before using other carriers. Freight costs are to be fixed at cost plus 15%.

AGGREMEX

The third joint venture company will be responsible for the sale and distribution of the aggregate once it arrives in the United States. It will sign long-term contracts with Quarimex for supply and with Cariston for transportation. It will make pricing and marketing decisions and will operate in three primary locations: Houston, New Orleans and Tampa.

The company's major activities have been:

1. The securing, maintenance and purchase, where necessary, of waterfront sites with access to deep water channels and close to inland transportation.

2. Completion of the contractual structure between itself, Quarimex and Cariston.

3. Detailed market analysis, pricing strategy etc.

4. US regulations and restrictions – there are several protectionist measures that apply to the importation of raw materials, one of which requires that 50% of any foreign source material used on Federal highways should be carried on US flagged ships. This has been met through the charter of the smaller carrier from CSL.

Market Demands

Within the target areas of Houston, New Orléans and Tampa, total sales of aggregate were over US$500m in 1986.

The project sales strategy is to be the low cost producer in a market where the existing suppliers have fundamental quality and resource limits and significant freight costs if supplies are to be found from elsewhere. A major market share will not be sought. Sales will begin on a limited scale, say 20% of the final volume, rising to 50% in the second year and reaching full project capacity in the ninth year.

Demand for Construction Aggregates
(millions of tons)

Actual	1970	1975	1980	1982	1984	1986
Houston	16	21	32	35	26	23
Tampa	10	11	14	12	17	18
New Orleans	9	8	8	9	9	8
Projected	*1988*	*1990*	*1992*	*1994*	*1996*	*1998*
Houston	23	27	33	33	32	34
Tampa	16	16	17	16	16	17
New Orleans	8	8	10	9	10	11

Sales Prices

Sales prices have tended to be stable in real terms around US$9.50 per ton with marginal fluctuations on either side. A continuation of these price levels is expected, although the present suppliers are expected to make significant price cuts during the first year or two of the project's entry as a deterrent. Thereafter prices are expected to assume the average level.

Sensitivity Analysis
This forecasts the variations of market price and the rate of build-up of sales volumes. The project is relatively insensitive to capital costs or increases in the variable cost of shipping. In the unlikely event that the sponsors were unsuccessful in penetrating the market to the extent assumed, and the purchase of the second bulk carrier was indefinitely postponed, the project would remain liquid and the debt service cover held at 1:1. The first carrier is due for delivery in 1989 and the second in 1992.

The project provides considerable and varied cost advantages over all of the traditional suppliers to this marketplace.

At this point, readers are asked to stop and consider the following questions:

1. **From the point of view of AMSTONE's relationship banker, is the proposed three company structure ideal?**

   If not, and given the broad risks, what alternatives would you suggest?

2. **The funding of the proposed operating companies has been put together piecemeal. You represent a multinational bank capable of cross border lending and control. What would have been the advantages for the bank if it had acted as lead manager for overall syndicated finance?**

Project Financing Requirements

International Finance Corporation (IFC), an affiliate of the World Bank, has been involved with both project sponsors, but particularly MEXICON with which it already has a strong relationship.

The financing lines are in place as shown in Appendix 1 and, in the case of Quarimex, the Mexican sources could include a subsidised export finance line from Banco de Mexico which is normally available to pre-finance exports of qualifying Mexican companies. Contingent funding arrangements are built in to cover potential over-runs, financial shortfalls or cashflow deficits until the project has proved its viability. In addition to the IFC lending as indicated on the schedule, the corporation will provide a guarantee to Cariston's commercial bank lenders of US$22m, i.e. one half of the original base capital cost of the bulk carriers. In this way it will adopt that risk on behalf of Mexicon, as commercial bankers are generally unwilling to increase their Mexican exposure. Amstone will guarantee its own 50% liability on base costs on behalf of Cariston.

The shortfall between the two guarantees and the total funding for Cariston will be secured by a charge over one of the two bulk carriers.

The lenders to Cariston have taken detailed advice from their specialist shipping unit as to the valuation of the bulk carriers in a forced sale.

Under normal circumstances, advances against vessels of this specialised nature would be calculated as a percentage of hull value to debt. This does *not* apply in this particular situation.

A review of the trends in valuation of 5 year old 60,000 DWT bulk carriers over the last few years, when there has been a limited market, shows:

Year	Value
1981	US$22m
1983	US$9.25m
1986	US$5.2m

The current price would be c.US$15m.

Project Assumptions
(see following tables)

Base Case

Revenues
Tons sold will be on the basis of gaining the forecast market share across Houston, Tampa and New Orleans.

Revenue per ton
Real revenue per ton is expected to grow through 1995 as the product mix improves and the higher quality aggregate is sold. Projected real revenue will grow at an annual 5% inflation rate.

Expenses
All expenses are expected to grow at a 5% inflation adjusted rate.

Worst Case

All of the assumptions made for the base case will continue with the exception of:

Tons sold and shipped
Tons sold will be reduced by 10% across the board.

Revenue per ton
The revenue per ton will no longer grow with the inflation factor.

Expenses
Expenses will continue to grow with the inflation factor. Fuel expenses will grow by US$5 per barrel.

GULF AGGREGATE PROJECT

BASE CASE

Income Statement
US$000's

	1987	1988	1989	1990	1991	1992	1993	1994	1995	1996	1997	1998	1999	2000	2001
NET REVENUES	—	—	12,620	27,591	34,042	54,201	72,792	85,022	92,137	99,018	111,825	127,016	134,203	141,978	147,869
Production costs	—	—	2,287	5,327	5,887	8,327	10,400	11,437	12,657	13,685	15,267	17,423	18,859	19,927	20,678
Gross Profit	—	—	10,333	22,264	28,155	45,874	62,392	73,585	79,480	85,333	96,558	109,593	115,344	122,051	127,191
OPERATING EXPENSES															
Quarimex															
Overheads	179	1,229	1,308	1,287	1,411	1,426	1,428	1,484	1,559	1,628	1,720	1,808	1,881	1,976	2,079
Carlston															
30,000 DWT Ship		—	—	591	673	1,395	1,787	2,894	2,269	3,181	3,401	3,695	3,787	3,989	4,233
60,000 DWT Ships		—	6,343	4,528	3,495	5,849	6,848	7,403	7,790	8,282	9,425	11,070	11,521	12,237	12,807
Overheads	241	234	431	605	742	1,095	1,151	1,224	1,283	1,341	1,408	1,483	1,560	1,637	1,717
Aggremex															
Overheads	81	978	1,473	1,647	1,912	2,108	2,360	2,495	2,637	2,786	2,947	3,147	3,322	3,490	3,657
Consolidated Op.															
Expenses	501	2,441	9,555	8,658	8,233	11,873	13,574	15,500	15,538	17,218	18,901	21,203	22,071	23,329	24,493
Interest Cover	-1.26	-1.26	-1.26	-1.41	2.10	3.91	6.91	9.92	14.12	20.20	34.12	52.36	67.25	87.68	115.88
Debt Service Cover						2.58	3.31	2.51	3.06	3.07	4.25	10.27	9.18	9.59	13.99

GULF AGGREGATE PROJECT

WORST CASE

Income Statement
US$000's

	1987	1988	1989	1990	1991	1992	1993	1994	1995	1996	1997	1998	1999	2000	2001
NET REVENUES	—	—	10,703	22,482	26,387	40,211	51,342	57,208	58,994	60,245	64,991	70,286	70,637	71,201	70,641
Production Costs	—	—	2,001	4,734	5,267	7,521	9,345	10,451	11,385	12,462	13,851	15,737	16,892	18,052	18,831
Gross Profit	—	—	8,702	17,748	21,120	32,690	41,997	46,757	47,609	47,783	51,140	54,549	53,745	53,149	51,810
OPERATING EXPENSES															
Quarimex															
Overheads	179	1,220	1,308	1,287	1,411	1,426	1,428	1,484	1,559	1,628	1,720	1,808	1,881	1,976	2,079
Cariston															
30,000 DWT Ship				591	673	1,395	1,787	2,894	2,269	3,181	3,401	3,695	3,737	3,989	4,233
60,000 DWT Ships			6,343	4,528	3,495	5,849	6,848	7,403	7,790	8,282	9,425	11,070	11,521	12,137	12,807
Overheads	241	234	431	605	742	1,095	1,151	1,224	1,283	1,341	1,408	1,483	1,550	1,637	1,717
Aggremex															
Overheads	81	978	1,473	1,647	1,912	2,108	2,360	2,495	2,637	2,786	2,947	3,147	3,322	3,490	3,657
Consolidated Op.															
Expenses	501	2,441	9,555	8,658	8,233	11,873	13,574	15,500	15,538	17,218	18,901	21,203	22,071	23,329	24,493
Interest Cover		-1.26	-1.50	0.57	1.04	1.86	3.39	4.49	5.98	7.46	11.66	16.61	19.03	21.39	23.91
Debt Service Cover						1.35	1.92	1.34	1.68	1.46	1.97	4.58	3.72	3.14	4.93

TASKS

1. Your multinational bank has been asked to organise the whole of the financing based upon the three-company structure.

   Consider:

   (a) The nature of the risks inherent in the overall project (i.e. as distinct from those to be addressed by each company against its own part of the operation).

   (b) The possible economic and political risks and whether these areas of sensitivity have been addressed by the sponsoring companies.

   (c) Whether the proposed financial structure given in Appendix 1 could be improved and, if so, how.

2. Your bank is to provide part of the funding for Quarimex.

   (a) Define the nature of the risks within the proposed production operation and consider whether they have been adequately addressed by the sponsors.

   (b) Every risk is worth its reward. Consider the interest rate margin decisions against the various funding lines.

3. Your bank is to provide the major funding line for the commissioning and building of the bulk carriers (see Appendix 1).

   Consider:

   (a) The risks in this sector of the operation and whether they have been adequately addressed by the sponsors.

   (b) The interest rate margin decisions against the various funding lines.

4. Your bank is to provide the relatively small facilities for Aggremex.

   (a) Define the nature of the risks and consider whether they have been adequately addressed by the sponsors.

   (b) Consider the interest rate margin decisions against the various funding lines.

Appendix 1 – Project Organisation

QUARIMEX	CARISTON	AGGREMEX
Joint Venture 51% MEXICON 49% AMSTONE Equity US$28m	Joint Venture 50% AMSTONE 50% MEXICON Equity US$3.5m	Joint Venture 51% AMSTONE 49% MEXICON Equity US$21.5m
ROLE	ROLE	ROLE
Quarry operation Port construction Port concession	Commission building of two 60,000 DWT bulk carriers – freight	Securing, maintaining port facilities – sale and distribution of aggregate

Finance Requirement and Sources
(US Dollars – Millions)

	QUARIMEX	CARISTON	AGGREMEX
Exim*	14.0	7.5	
IFC	7.3		5.3
Mexican Sources	19.9		
Commercial Banks		61.1	
Others	.7	.5	1.1
TOTAL	41.9	69.1	6.4

*Export-Import Bank of the United States.

Appendix 2 – The Joint Venture Companies

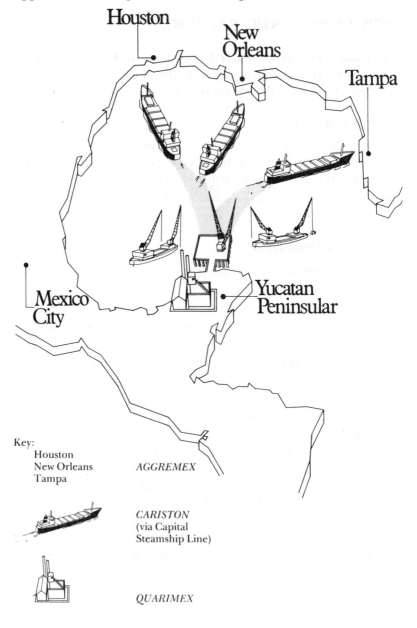

Key:

Houston
New Orleans   *AGGREMEX*
Tampa

CARISTON
(via Capital
Steamship Line)

QUARIMEX

DISCUSSION SYLLABUS 1

RISK IN DOMESTIC BANKING

The nature of the risks undertaken in domestic banking – current and prospective changes – their implications in the future for products, policies and business results.

Aims of Discussion

(a) In the light of recent and anticipated trends in the market-place, to assess the present and future importance of credit risk and the methods for its measurement and control.

(b) To examine the changing and increasing impact of non-credit risks on banks.

Factors to be Considered

1. *Assessing the Balance Between Risk and Reward*

    (a) Continuing importance of profitability, including its relevance to maintaining adequate capital.

    (b) Increased competition and developments in the pattern of competition.

    (c) New opportunities for business and the attendant risks.

    (d) Recent experience in credit and other losses.

2. *New Products/Off Balance Sheet Items*

    (a) Commercial Paper (including the growth in the Sterling Commercial Paper market) – Note Issuance Facilities (NIFs), Revolving Underwriting Facilities (RUFs), Multi-Option Facilities (MOFs), Exchange Rate Agreements (ERAs), Forward Rate Agreements (FRAs) etc.

    (b) Currency and interest rate swaps; 'caps and collars' etc.; over-the-counter and traded options.

    (c) Increasing demand for non-recourse and off-balance-sheet finance.

    (d) Daylight exposure.

3. *Operational Non-Credit Risks and Other Factors*

   (a) Fraud and forgery, including plastic card and computer fraud.

   (b) Reliance on technology and the consequences of operational breakdowns.

   (c) Staff poaching/head hunting – systems, customers' defection etc.

   (d) Supervisory (Bank of England, Securities and Investment Board etc.) and change of accounting standards (e.g. Accounting Standards Committee Exposure Draft 42, March 1988 – "Accounting for Special Purpose Transactions").

   (e) Government intervention – possibility of 'credit squeeze', direct or indirect, nationalisation.

Questions

1. The banks have been prepared to accept a wider range of domestic credit risks in recent years. Are all these risks measured and assessed appropriately? If not, what changes should be made to the way in which the banks undertake this task in future?

2. Considerable time and effort are expended on examining and controlling credit risks. What other major risks within the domestic operations of a bank are most in need of similar examination?

3. What factors ultimately limit the total risks which a bank can safely accept, and whose responsibility is it to assess these factors?

DISCUSSION SYLLABUS 2

RISK IN INTERNATIONAL BANKING

Until recently, risk management meant almost entirely credit management and the banks had strong credit skills. Today risk management is a much wider issue.

Aims of Discussion

(a) To identify and analyse key areas of risk in international banking.

(b) To consider how those risks should be measured.

(c) To appreciate the environmental changes that dictate a different risk management approach.

(d) To consider ways of improving a bank's management systems so as to improve risk management without reducing profitability.

Factors to be Considered

1. *The Globalisation of Markets*

   (a) Emergence of new competitors; relative competitive positions.

   (b) Increased pace of activity in financial markets.

   (c) The impact of a reduced number of countries with acceptable risk.

   (d) The introduction of new products.

   (e) The amalgamation of banks and securities firms.

2. *Specific Types of Risk*

   (a) Position risks arising from trading operations.

   (b) Liquidity risks in funding activities internationally and the potential impact of off balance sheet transactions.

(c) Depth of markets in trading financial instruments; under-writing risk.

(d) The credit risk associated with international banking pro-ducts and the measurement/monitoring of that risk.

(e) Risks of reliance on cross border payment and clearing systems.

(f) Operational risks associated with international operations, e.g. political, regulatory and fraud.

Questions

1. International banks today face all the risks described above. Which of those risks could cripple a bank? What specific action can be taken to reduce them?

2. What aspects of technology pose the greatest risk to the banks?

3. Does the current international debt crisis mean an end to new loans to less developed countries? What have we learned from the old loans?

READING LIST

1. Bank capital and risk, by Bernard Wesson. *The Chartered Institute of Bankers*, 1985.

2. Bank strategy in an age of rapid change, by Wilfried Guth. *The Banker*, April 1986.

3. Capital adequacy, by Peter Wood. *The Treasurer*, September 1987.

4. Changes in large corporate banking, by Sir Jeremy Morse. *The Treasurer*, April 1988.

5. Country risk assessment: Swiss Bank Corporation's approach. *Economic and Financial Prospects*, February/March 1988.

6. Credit assessment in Britain, by Margaret Hughes. *TSB Review*, November 1987.

7. International debt: the next stage, by David Lomax. *Banking World*, July 1987.

8. Ironing out those troublesome bumps, by Michael Blanden. *The Banker*, February 1988.

9. Managing transaction exposure: the Hertz approach, by Michael Bryant. *The Treasurer*, March 1987.

10. Multiple-option facilities. *Bank of England Quarterly Bulletin*, May 1988.

11. Operating under a regulatory environment, by Michael Beales. *The Treasurer*, September 1987.

12. Personal credit in perspective. *Bank of England Quarterly Bulletin*, February 1988.

13. A review of interest rate risk management techniques, by Tim Goode. *The Treasurer*, November 1987.

14. Risk: taking the temperature and finding a cure, by Peter S. Rose. *Canadian Banker*, November-December 1987.

15. Risk asset ratios, by Davis Lomax. *The Treasurer*, September 1987.

16. Risk management: more than just managing risk, by Jens Nielsen. *Banker International,* April 1988.

17. Supervision and the bank treasurer, by Robin Leigh-Pemberton. *The Treasurer,* September 1987.

18. Tax aspects of international treasury planning. by Derek Ross. *The Treasurer,* January 1987.

Recommended Further Reading

19. Back to the country risk, by Ephraim A. Clark. *International Correspondent Banker,* September 1987.

20. Country risk: assessment and monitoring. 2nd ed. by Thomas Krayenbuehl. *Woodhead-Faulkner,* 1988.
    See Chapter 14: New lending to countries in difficult financial situations.

21. Country risk analysis, by John Calverley. *Butterworths,* 1985.
    See Chapter 1: Defining country risk.
    Chapter 2: The risks and their costs to banks.
    Chapter 3: Willingness versus ability to pay.

22. Domestic and international banking, by M .K. Lewis and K. T. Davis. *Philip Allan,* 1987.
    See Chapter 1: Modern banking.

23. Forecasting U.K. interest rates, by Mark Brett. *The Treasurer,* November 1987.

24. Managing economic exposure: a consultant's view, by Roger Edmunds and Graham Bond. *The Treasurer,* February 1987.

25. The risk calculators, by John Paul Lee. *International Correspondent Banker,* November 1987.

26. Securitization in the retail banking world, by Jack W. Aber. *Journal of Retail Banking,* Spring 1988.

27. U.K. banking supervision, evolution, practice and issues, edited by E. P. M. Gardener. *Allen & Unwin,* 1986.
    See Chapter 1.

The Chartered Institute of Bankers

Cambridge Seminar
Programme

4–9 September 1988

The Banks and Risk Management

Sunday
4 September

20.30–21.45 Plenary briefing session followed by informal discussion in syndicates

Monday
5 September

08.45–12.30 THE CENTRAL BANKER'S VIEW Rodney Galpin, FCIB, Chairman Designate, Standard Chartered Bank

14.30–16.00 Discussion 1 (Syndicates)

16.30–18.00 Discussion 1 Plenary Session

20.30 After dinner presentation on the management of Christ's College

Tuesday
6 September

08.45–12.30 RISK IN DOMESTIC BANKING John Brooks FCIB, Deputy Group Chief Executive, Midland Bank Plc

14.30–18.00 Case Study

20.30–21.30 Informal discussion

Wednesday
7 September

08.45–12.30 RISK IN INTERNATIONAL BANKING – A CORPORATE TREASURER'S VIEW John Robins, Director of Finance and Management Services, Willis Faber Plc

14.30–17.30 Case Study Plenary Session

20.30–21.30 Discussion 2 (Syndicates)

Thursday
8 September

08.45–12.30 RISK IN INTERNATIONAL BANKING – A BANKER'S VIEW Dr Thomas Krayenbuehl, Senior Vice President, Union Bank of Switzerland

14.30–16.30 Discussion 2 Plenary Session followed by debate

18.45 Reception

19.30 Farewell Dinner

Friday
9 September

Morning Depart

PREVIOUS CAMBRIDGE SEMINARS

Year	*Theme*	*Director*
1968	The Future of British Banking	Henry Eason
1969	Bank Management – Recruitment and Training	Henry Eason
1971	The Marketing of Bank Services	Geoffrey Dix
1972	Banking for Profit	Eric Glover
1974	The Banks and Society	David Whelpton
1975	The Branch Banker: Today and Tomorrow	Geoffrey Dix
1976	The Banks and Industry	Eric Glover
1977	Banks and the British Exporter	David Whelpton
1978	The Banks and Small Businesses	George Walters
1980	The Banks and their Competitors*	Eric Glover
1981	The Banks and the Public*	Peter Spiro
1982	The Banks and Technology in the 1980s*	Eric Glover
1983	The Banks and Personal Customers*	Alan Miller, FCIB
1984	Financing New Technology*	Don Fiddes, FCIB
1986	Bank Strategies for the 1990s*	George Walters
1987	Banking Through the Looking Glass*	Robert Rendel

In 1970, 1973, 1979 and 1985, the Institute was host to the International Banking Summer School, and seminars were not held in those years.

*Papers still available from the Institute.